D1563677

Where Yet the Sweet Birds Sing

Where Yet the Sweet Birds Sing

Richard Quinney

Borderland Books

Published by Borderland Books, Madison, WI
www.borderlandbooks.net

Publisher's Cataloging-in-Publication Data
Quinney, Richard.
  Where yet the sweet birds sing / Richard Quinney — 1st ed.
    p. : photos. ; cm.
    ISBN - 10: 0-9768781-0-0
    ISBN - 13: 978-0-9768781-0-0
  1. Quinney, Richard — Diaries. 2. Quinney, Richard — Homes
and haunts — Wisconsin — Walworth County. 3. Nature.
4. Spiritual biography — United States. 5. Cancer — Patients —
Diaries. I. Title.
PS3567.U53 W45 2006
818.6   2005904608

Printed in the United States of America
First edition

That time of year thou mayst in me behold
When yellow leaves, or none, or few, do hang
Upon those boughs which shake against the cold,
Bare ruined choirs, where late the sweet birds sang.

William Shakespeare

Sonnet 73

Contents

Preface

WRITING — especially the fairly regular keeping of a journal — has been a part of my life for years. Early in my adult life, I developed the need to make sense of my life as lived daily. Important also has been the use of photography to see and understand the world. This book is a continuation of these forces and habits in my life. I hope that my accounting will be of help to others in the living of their lives.

The disease — chronic lymphocytic leukemia — that had been quietly progressing for twelve years finally revealed itself in swellings, fever, and fatigue. A lab test found that the primary cells in defense of infection had disappeared from my body. The disease had reached the stage at which treatment could be attempted. I would be in the hospital for weeks, and I would have rounds of chemotherapy and infusions of monoclonal antibodies. All of the next year would be an odyssey as attempts were made to control the disease and as I, with the help of family and friends, lived with the great uncertainty of life and death. Throughout the year, I would keep a close watch.

The pilgrimage is near at hand. In the living of each day. If this pilgrim were to use religious terms, he would say that God is in the details. Resources more existential than esoteric in nature are called for. Any wisdom of the wholeness of reality is realized only in life itself. The trials and transformations of the past year have affirmed a simple conclusion: Life is more precious than we can ever imagine. Although my fairly solitary mode of existence continues, I value more than ever discourse in the larger world.

Just as our lives are always and inevitably changing, our life stories are changing. All of us continuously alter and revise our life stories as we live. There are times when we are between stories, when the stories of our lives are in transition, when we are creating new stories or revising old ones. When we are uncertain about the direction of our lives and how we might live. And there are those fortunate times when we open ourselves to what is actually going on, giving complete attention to the reality of all things.

During the odyssey of the year 2001 that I chronicle, the year that my illness was being treated, and being treated experimentally, I gave close attention to my daily life. The new century had brought me to retirement from a lifetime of teaching and professing. I had yet to know how I might live a life beyond employment. And my wife and I were in the process of deciding where we might live, requiring a move to another place. But as the year progressed, we began to spend more time at the farm. This is the farm that has belonged to my family for generations, since first being settled by my great-grandparents emigrating from Ireland

during the famine of the 1840s. This is the farm of my birth
and growing up years. It is the place from which I fled to
make my own life, but it is the place to which I have always
returned out of need.

It would be easy to think of the farm more in the past
tense than in the present. To think of it, as Shakespeare
wrote in his sonnet, as the place "where late the sweet
birds sang." But as the recent summer progressed, and as I
went to the farm weekly, I came to know the farm in present terms. Although there were the strong and constant
reminders of the past—from the rot and the rust of decay-
ing buildings to the aging artifacts found in drawers and
trunks—I was transported by the wonders of the present in
this much-loved place. With the coming of fall and winter,
I continued to find solace in what is here and now.

The account that follows—chronicled each month of
the year—is a documentation of, and a witnessing to, the
living of a life. And the lives of others near and dear to me.
In the course of this odyssey, in the course of the tale I tell
during the passing of the year, we made our move from one
place to another. Still, we are still close to the farm. Where
yet the sweet birds sing.

January

W E START FROM HOME. Along the way, as we get older, as T. S. Eliot writes in his poem "East Coker": "The world becomes stranger, the pattern more complicated." Our lifetime now burns in every moment, and not only the lifetime of each one of us, "but of old stones that cannot be deciphered." We continue to be explorers.

The thermometer outside the kitchen window has hovered around zero the last several days. My health — or the lack of it — has kept me indoors. On Christmas morning, I opened the front door, and with my back to the sun, pointed the binoculars toward a sheet of white paper, and an image of a partial solar eclipse formed before us. Solveig and I watched as the moon's shadow passed over the face of the sun. For a few moments, the sparkling snow blanketing the front yard turned to blue.

The night before winter solstice — a night with a wind chill of minus forty degrees — a small screech owl fell down the chimney and into the burning fireplace. Immediately it flew out of the flame and into the living room, landing gracefully on the banister of the stairway. We all gazed carefully at one another. After a while we coaxed the owl toward the doorway, and it flew out the opened door. We wondered later why we had not spent more time together. We had wanted, I suppose, to see the owl safely returned to the night.

This new-year morning we woke up in the bedroom of the farmhouse. We watched the sun rise over the wooded hills and the snow-covered fields. Long icicles were hanging from the roof of the barn. The branches of the trees surrounding the house, covered with an icing during the night, glistened in the morning light. For a good part of the day, driving in all directions, we meandered over the snow-packed backroads that finally led south toward home.

EACH TIME THAT I go to the hospital for a lab test, I replay in my mind a song composed by Billy Strayhorn and recorded by Duke Ellington. "Blood Count" was written by Strayhorn as he was undergoing treatment in upper Manhattan for his own blood disease. A good share of the emotions of being ill and being treated — with all the uncertainties — are contained in "Blood Count."

Yesterday's test at the University of Wisconsin Hospital in Madison found my white blood count at a low and my precious neutrophils sliding down to 1000 again. I am hoping for an improvement of counts as the Rituxan treatments take hold, as they did three months ago. The weekly trips north are being driven through weather that would otherwise keep us at home.

WHAT WOULD DAILY LIFE be like if one imagined one-self as being Charles Darwin on the five-year voyage of the Beagle? You would be occupying the cramped rear cabin of the ship. Sitting at a table, you would be writing in a journal about the voyage that would set the pattern for the rest of your life. Occasionally you would go ashore, and in a notebook record your explorations and discoveries. In spite of seasickness, you would continue the journey with enthusiasm and deliberation.

I think of myself lately as a naturalist on the voyage of the Beagle. Just before my illness reached the stage for treatment, Solveig and I flew to London to spend three weeks in a rented flat in Chelsea. We made several day trips from London to visit the home of Charles Darwin, to explore the place that Darwin lived the last forty years of his life. I imagined Darwin sitting at his desk in the dark study on the northeast side of Down House, writing a book on the origin of species.

We walked the Sandwalk, the path that Darwin had constructed, a path he had covered with sand from a pit in the woods. At mid-day, regardless of the weather, Darwin would stroll around the Sandwalk, the woods on one side of the path and the meadow on the other. We are told in various accounts that these daily walks were constitutional, but that they were also the source of much of Darwin's creative thought. I picked up a small stone, a lime-covered flint stone from the edge of the path, and placed it in my pocket.

The stone rests now, clearly labeled, at the edge of my writing desk.

A FOG THIS MORNING signals a warming of the landscape and the coming of a January thaw. Snow on the roof of the house is melting and falling to the ground. I must find a way to clear the frozen and leaf-filled gutters and downspouts.

The *New York Times* confirms the report that these winter months across the United States have been the coldest on record. A meteorologist is quoted as saying that "folks in the upper Midwest who lived through this December will have stories to tell their grandchildren — and unlike most stories, they'll be backed up by data." Additional cold outbreaks are predicted through March, but in the middle of January we are finding relief from the long cold spell.

I finally asked my doctor the prognosis for my illness — for my life. He told me that there could be no prognosis, that my illness is unique and that no prediction can be offered. Likely it will be an infection that will bring me down. An infection that cannot be resisted by my impaired immune system. I asked if this would be a good time for a trip — to Florida, perhaps. In a light-hearted manner, my doctor said that I should "make hay while the sun shines." This morning I waver between making hay and packing up a life.

A NEWSLETTER ARRIVED in the mail from a religious community in town. An older couple—older than I am—report on the health problems resulting from an auto accident. They refer to their convalescence as a wonderful adventure and a meaningful experience. Although I have been told that I am courageous, I have not yet developed the notion that I am on an adventure or that I am having a meaningful experience. I may come to think otherwise, eventually.

When I asked my doctor for a prognosis, he told me that I had nearly died when I was hospitalized three months ago. I was without neutrophils and there seemed to be no way to restore them, and I had pneumonia. I am living now with no prognosis, and a near-death experience. And I feel weak and fatigued and have aches and pains. What meaning is there in the ending of the only life I know?

ONCE, NOT SO LONG AGO, I was a pilgrim. I thought of myself as being a pilgrim on a long journey. I was searching for the meaning of life. Eventually, with meditation and practice, I found that the meaning of life is simply in the living of life. Such meaning of life depends, of course, on being alive, on not being dead.

On my pilgrimage, I learned the ancient Vedic and Buddhist wisdom that all things are one. The quest gradually changed, however, from the desire for things not seen to an appreciation of all that is concrete and already here. The living of each day with some degree of attention and awareness replaced the pilgrimage to higher realms.

This is not to say that the earlier quest — and the travel to sacred places — is irrelevant to my life. The consciousness developed in that quest provides the grounding for my life today. But there is nothing like an illness — the failing of the body — to bring you to the existentials of life. Resources beyond the pilgrimage are called for: science and medicine, clinical care, love and friendship, courage, and the skill to be alone. Life itself is quite enough, as long as there is life. Still, you wonder, without life, what then?

THE RED SQUIRREL has been safely removed from the bottom of the chimney. The man from Animal Control enticed it into the cage and released it live in a woods far away. A wire netting has been attached to the top of the chimney to prevent further invasions of wildlife into the house. We species must maintain and secure our habitats.

As is my habit, and solace, I am at my desk again this morning. A few words are being offered to the pages of my journal. Some days my only accomplishments are the few words written in my journal, words that direct me to the day and to my life. Today I report — in addition to the capture and release of the squirrel — my reading of the new translation of the *Bhagavad Gita* by Stephen Mitchell. For

years I have turned to one translation or another of the Gita
when the question "How should I live?" has become press-
ing. The Gita instructs us to go beyond the separate self, to
center ourselves in the deathless reality that is at the core
of our being. The whole world — now and ever — is our
home. With this wisdom, as Mitchell notes, "we come to a
place where dualities such as sacred and profane, spiritual
and unspiritual, fall away as well." Thus my indifference of
late to religious debates, to religion itself. Everything essen-
tial is already present within us — to be discovered when
necessary.

THERE IS A WORLD OUTSIDE — an outside world —
that is to be acknowledged. Last night President Clinton
delivered his farewell address to the nation. The inaugura-
tion of George W. Bush takes place tomorrow in Washington.
The Beat poet Gregory Corso has died. There are power
blackouts in California. Cold air is moving south from
Canada. I know: the *New York Times* is delivered to my
doorstep each morning. Meanwhile, this tiredness within
me persists.

In the new translation of the Gita, the familiar passages
are presented:

> Death is certain for the born:
> for the dead, rebirth is certain.

Since both cannot be avoided,
You have no reason for your sorrow.

Before birth, beings are unmanifest
between birth and death, manifest;
at death, unmanifest again.
What cause for grief is all this?

Abstractly, intellectually, the ancient wisdom is readily accepted. Concretely, in everyday life, I have yet to show no grief for the unmanifest. I long especially now for the manifest I knew in my mother and father, and I wish to retain the manifest I know in myself.

AS IS OUR HABIT LATELY, we read aloud to each other in bed before turning out the light. Reading only a few pages a night, we have completed Willa Cather's *The Professor's House.* Near the end of the novel, the professor, Godfrey St. Peter, recalls the person that he was once, originally: the solitary youth. That boy is remembered, and perhaps can be only recognized in aging and, in Cather's vision, in death. In the course of the professor's adult life and career, Cather writes, "a new creature was grafted into the original one." She then describes the following epiphany:

What he had not known was that, at a given time,
that first nature could return to a man, unchanged
by all the pursuits and passions and experiences of
his life; untouched even by the tastes and intellectual
activities which have been strong enough to give him
distinction among his fellows and to have made for
him, as they say, a name in the world. Perhaps this
reversion did not often occur, but he knew it had
happened to him … He did not regret his life, but he
was indifferent to it. It seemed to him like the life of
another person.

I think of my own life, of course, as we read the last
pages of *The Professor's House.* Certainly I do not feel an
indifference to my adult years, as did Professor St. Peter.
Although I may have some feeling of an ending, I have a
sense of fulfillment and, especially, a sense of continuity. All
my life I have known that my original nature was that of
one who was born on a farm in the Midwest. I grew up on
the farm, was nurtured and guided by my parents, worked
in the fields with my brother, drove to high school in the
pickup truck, and left home for college and the life that
would follow. True, I sought an identity that would take me
beyond the farm, even eliminating one of my given names
to signal the change. I sought a larger world. But all the
time, I knew I was the person that my mother had photo-
graphed sitting on the grain binder behind the team of

horses. On the back of the photograph, my mother wrote: "Our new grain binder, 1937. How Earl loved to ride."

TO THE FAR NORTH, the first sign of spring. The darkness of the arctic night will end today as the sun rises above the horizon for the first time since November. The amount of sunshine will increase at least nine minutes each day. For us to the south, the arctic sunrise is the beginning of a process that will modify the bitter air masses that have been reaching us for several weeks. The mid-winter ebb, and I must contact a plumber today to advise me on installing a sump pump in the basement. All precautions have to be taken to prevent the growth of mold in the house. A sump pump might give aid to my immune system.

Why does one — why do I — make a record of these daily activities? There are many reasons: to recognize the significance of everyday life; to keep track of my life and my thoughts and feelings, and how they change with the days; to bring me to an awareness of what is going on around me and within me; to keep me in contact with the larger world; to make a record that may be of use to others as they live their own lives; to inform my family of an interior life that is often beyond the words of discourse. And like the Ancient Mariner of Coleridge's poem, there is the tale I need to tell.

It took a crisis in the personal life of Charles Darwin to convince him of the need to begin a diary. His biographer,

Janet Browne, observes: "Faced with a long voyage, fully aware that a new kind of shipboard adventure was starting, emotions at bursting point, painfully conscious that he was stepping out into an unknown world without his usual solicitous empire of family and friends, Darwin plainly believed the occasion should not pass unmarked." In the course of keeping his diary, "he began to create himself as the man who joined the Beagle expedition." All of his life, Darwin would record his observations in diaries, notebooks, journals, and in an autobiography late in his life. To a great extent, his idea of life was the solitary act of writing it down.

TODAY is the Chinese New Year, the first day of the Year of the Snake. This was just announced by Garrison Keillor on the morning's edition of "The Writer's Almanac."

The conditions and crises that bring one to writing are many, and vary greatly from one person to another. Yesterday I completed my reading of the second volume of Victor Klemperer's *I Will Bear Witness*. The book is the recently translated diary that Klemperer kept in Germany for the years 1942 through 1945. Klemperer, as a Jew, with the minimal protection of being married to an Aryan, lived in Dresden during the Nazi war years. Each day there are the dangers of being searched, of hunger, of hard labor, of illness without proper care, of the apartment being raided, and of transport to a concentration camp.

His detailed diary entries often end with an observation such as this: "Why think any further? The future is completely dark, the end, one way or another, is close." The entry for a Saturday morning in April 1942 begins: "Each day brings a change for the worse in the general Jewish situation and in our particular situation, and each day I feel my heart failing more and more." Klemperer writes in his diary with great risk to his life, and he knows that he is bearing witness to his times.

> After the search I found several books, which had been taken off the shelf, lying on the desk. If one of them had been the Greek dictionary, if the manuscript pages had fallen out and had thus aroused suspicion, it would undoubtedly have meant my death. One is murdered for lesser misdemeanors. So these parts will go today. But I shall go on writing. That is my heroism. I will bear witness, precise witness!

Klemperer's forebodings are metaphysical as much as they are about being terrorized by the Gestapo. For there is the fear of complete extinction of himself. "Even if I survive Hitler, how much will still be left of me? It is so stupid: I fear non-existence, nothing else." At the end of December 1944, he writes: "I am incapable of somehow becoming reconciled to the thought of death; religious and philosophical

consolations are completely denied me. It is solely a matter
of maintaining one's dignity until the very end." Surviving
the war years, Klemperer regains his life as a university professor and continues to write until his death in 1960.

For me — five times around the indoor track at the
Recreation Center is equal to a mile. I try to take the walk
at least every other day. And I do a few stretches on two or
three of the exercise machines. I seem to be feeling stronger
this week. "More like my old self," I tell Solveig.

A GENTLE SNOW falls today. The lone squirrel forages at
the bird feeder in the back yard, its mate released by Animal
Control somewhere in yonder woods. A major earthquake
has struck in India during the night. At home, letters have
to be written and e-mail messages answered.

I go about reporting the truth — as I am knowing it.
Knowing, as Laurie Lee said in his autobiographical book *I
Can't Stay Long,* "that there is no pure truth, only moody
accounts of witnesses." I go about leaving these uncertain
messages for others.

No wonder that Ned Rorem titled his latest diary *Lies.* "If
I have learned one thing in the three-plus decades of publish-
ing diaries, it's that there is no universal accord, nor even a
recorded experience that I myself, the day after, can concur
with exactly." All is "Rashomon," Rorem says, alluding to
the Japanese film of the 1950s that has been so important

to my life and my career. "And virtually every event I've ever described in printed prose," Rorem adds, "has been proclaimed skewed by friends and foes alike." We compose in the heat of the fray—without benefit of foresight or hindsight. To be in the moment—in the sheer act of writing—is the essence of the daily entry. We stop time.

THE SABBATH, the day that always has my attention. Late afternoon, and snow is beginning to fall. We are listening to Nanci Griffith's new rendition of "Desperadoes Waiting for a Train," a song written by Guy Clark. A good metaphor, this title, for life as we know it. We are desperadoes waiting for a train.

Despite my turning away from anything organized as religion, my life is unavoidably spiritual. And in spite of other intentions, my longing is for immortality. This mind knows only that it cannot know the ultimate meaning of existence. For years I have been enlightened by the advice of the Zen master Seung Sahn, given in letters to his students: "So I hope you only go straight—don't know, and keep the great bodhisattva vow, get enlightenment, and save all beings from suffering." We only don't know.

THE CASUALTY RATE from the earthquake in India keeps rising. Estimates of the numbers reach as high as twenty thousand. Hundreds of thousands are homeless and, as the *New York Times* describes conditions, "now are living beside small fires under a cold winter sky." Survivors of a quake such as this "have lost faith, perhaps forever, in the firmness of earth itself." Much of human suffering is Shiva's dancing.

WE ARE WHAT WE GIVE OUR ATTENTION TO. To understand someone is to observe what that person attends to daily. What we see, what we think about, and what we do are signs of who we are, of what we care for, and of what we love.

We thus give our attention to the details of everyday life. In *Zen Mind, Beginner's Mind,* Shunryu Suzuki observes:

> When we hear the sound of the pine trees on a windy
> day, perhaps the wind is just blowing, and the pine
> tree is just standing in the wind. That is all that they
> are doing. But the people who listen to the wind
> in the tree will write a poem, or will feel something
> unusual.

At the end of my street flows a river that passes a lagoon ringed with willows. A bridge, winter's snow, a tree with a lone crow, buildings of stone, and a river flowing. Bridge over the East Lagoon.

February

Another blast of arctic air surges south through the northern parts of the Plains and the Mississippi Valley. Here, west of Chicago, it is too cold to take a morning's walk downtown. Again, my travels must be close to home.

At home—but I have been a wanderer all my life. No wonder that I am fascinated with Coleridge's Ancient Mariner. And like the Ancient Mariner, my tale of adventure must be told to anyone who passes by. The perfect myth for keeping a journal. An atonement, something for shooting the red-tailed hawk that once soared over the fields at the farm.

My tale I tell, my tale I teach, to any student who will listen. To tell of things, all things, both great and small.

A WEEKEND AT THE FARM. We drove the sixty miles north Saturday morning, and we returned at dawn this morning. All week a gray and white winter landscape, an austere beauty over the land that makes the spirit rise and fall all at once. The home country.

How many times have I contemplated moving back to the farm? I constantly think about the possibility, and I constantly reject it. How many people can return to the room where they slept as children? How many friends and acquaintances, as well as strangers, have I stopped to tell my tale of growing up on the farm in Wisconsin? I have become the Mariner of the Fields. In a way, I have never left the farm.

And now I learn that farmers have a higher rate of chronic lymphocytic leukemia (CLL) than other workers. The use of chemicals on land and animals is the likely cause of the leukemia. I would work all day in the fields — spring, summer, and fall — from the time I was very young to the time I left for college. One day, finally, I told my father, as I was shoveling my car out of a snowdrift in the driveway, "I'm leaving this godforsaken place and I'm never coming back."

I did come back, of course, many times — physically, mentally, and spiritually. I will never leave the farm. The farm that gave me birth is the farm that will give me death.

ONE IS FORTUNATE to find the words written by a loved one. Whether the words are on a postcard sent home, a few travel notes made on a trip, or a diary written long ago. I cherish the written words that are on the cards and letters I found in a cabinet on the front porch of the farmhouse.

At the age of twenty-four, in the year 1924, my father had written to his sister, his aunt, and his father during his trip to California. On the road, he wrote to his sister Marjorie:

> We meet cars from every state on the Lincoln
> Highway. Only a couple from Wisconsin. Lots of
> tourists at the tourist camps. About 15 cars here
> tonight. We use our pillows twenty-four hours each
> day. Sleep on them at night. Sit on them all day. We
> intend to get to Salt Lake City in about three days but
> you won't have time to write us there. And we don't
> know which trail we will take from there. But in case
> of sickness or anything like that a telegram would
> find us at the tourist camp. Had a chance to get a job
> with a threshing gang. Will close and make our bed.
> As ever, your brother.

Six months later, before returning home for spring work on the farm, my father wrote that he would never forget this trip and that "one could never tell you the sights without seeing them with your own eyes." I also found in the cabinet on the porch the negatives of the photographs that he took on his travel to California and back.

I was told by my mother, the year before she died, that she had kept a diary when she was a young girl. I asked if I might read the diary that begins in 1916 when she was nine years old. She said that not much happened in those days, that I could look at the diary some other time. Now, after two years, I read the words she wrote long ago:

> I took my camera to school. Teacher showed me how
> to take a picture. Teacher took a picture of me. Jack
> (my cat) would not hold still so I could not take his
> picture. We went to Millard and back in the car. I
> wore my hat to school.

On another day, my mother wrote: "Went to Elkhorn and bought a dish for mama and a handkerchief for papa and an eraser, tablet and composition book. Had dinner at the hotel."

My father and mother met at a dance in Delavan on a Saturday night in the fall of 1929. They married the next year and moved into the new farmhouse. I was born on a day in May in 1934, and my brother was born two years later. My father and mother stayed on the farm for the rest of their lives.

In a box on a high shelf in the closet I keep the letters my mother and father wrote to me after I left home. Occasionally I bring the box down and open it on my desk and read a few of the letters. I read the letters whenever I need to hear their voices, whenever I need to be reminded that they are still with me, whenever I need to know that death is not an ending.

THE TEXT FOR THIS SUNDAY MORNING is from the
new book *Lifelines* by a physician, Muriel Gillick, who spe-
cializes in the care of the elderly. The text follows a paragraph on the importance of remaining active and creative
no matter how weak and infirm we may be.

> Older people also need to feel part of something
> larger than themselves. One of the quintessential
> features of being human is the awareness and fear
> of mortality, and those who are frail are exquisitely
> conscious of the imminence of death. People need
> "immortality projects" to sustain themselves in the
> face of their earthly transience.

The immortality projects can include such activities as
writing books, helping others, and caring for one's children
and grandchildren. The crucial objective is to devote oneself
to something larger than this individual self. The end of our
exploration is to arrive where we started, and to know that
we are an integral part of the larger and infinite world. This
individual, particular self is contained in all that is universal.

Yes, the project, now late in life, is the "immortality project," a project that sustains us in the face of our earthly tran-
sience. Everything we mortals experience changes and passes
on. The ancient texts teach us, however, to know the ultimate
that does not change. To realize that we are that, the whole of
reality, *tat tvam asi:* Thou art that.

THE BLOOD COUNTS are better than they were two weeks ago. I continue to take the Augmentin pills for an apparent infection. The other aches and pains may be the consequence of previous treatments. A CT scan is being scheduled for me at the hospital; my doctors are making their own explorations. If the blood counts hold, and if I can pass the investigations, a winter trip to Florida may be possible after all. We have the airplane tickets in our hands. First-time snow birds.

SIX PLUMP DOVES rest on the limbs of the redbud in the backyard. I listen to the sound of water dripping from the roof of the house. Yellow, dry leaves cling to the branches of the Japanese maple. Patches of earth and lawn emerge from the slowly melting cover of snow. A gray sky. Fog and occasional flurries. With Valentine heart, I wait my love's return.

THE WAYS ARE MANY in the keeping of a journal. The motivations and the needs are various. But at the heart of my effort is a single reason — a paradox, seemingly, at first: to study oneself is to forget oneself, to become part of that which is larger than the individual self. This is the insight of Buddhism that informs my life daily. Expressed concisely by Shunryu Suzuki in *Zen Mind, Beginner's Mind:*

The purpose of studying Buddhism is to study ourselves and to forget ourselves. When we forget ourselves, we actually are the true activity of the big existence, or reality itself. When we realize this fact, there is no problem whatsoever in this world, and we can enjoy our life without feeling any difficulties. The purpose of our practice is to be aware of this fact.

I will enter for the record a paragraph from Suzuki's commentary on the way of Zen, a paragraph that can be read as the core reason for keeping a journal. The journal, the daily entry made at the quiet of a table or a desk, is basic practice.

Each one of us must make his own true way, and when we do, that way will express the universal way. This is the mystery. When you understand one thing through and through, you understand everything. When you try to understand everything, you will not understand anything. The best way is to understand yourself, and then you will understand everything. So when you try hard to make your own way, you will help others, and you will be helped by others. Before you make your own way you cannot help anyone, and no one can help you. To be independent in this true sense, we have to forget everything which we have in our mind and discover something quite new and different moment after moment. This is how we live in this world.

In the keeping of the journal, in understanding yourself, you are able to understand other things, and you are able to help others. A way of being in the world.

I SIT HERE with a box full of aging photographs retrieved from a cabinet in the living room of the farmhouse. The photographs are of my ancestors and those they knew as friends and neighbors. Photographs of people removed from me — if removed is the right word — by generations. A photograph of my grandfather, my father's father, a tall man in overalls standing in front of a barn. My mother's horse and cutter hitched to a post beside the milkhouse. The three brothers of my great-grandmother standing in a driveway in suits and vests. Marjorie, my father's sister — who died in mid-life of a ruptured appendix — holding a stem of lilacs down at the old place. A childhood photograph of my brother and me standing beside our grandfather's barn on the hill.

I have finished reading Martin Amis's memoir, titled *Experience*. The book closes with a line that I heard him read last May in an auditorium in London: "The parents are going, the children are staying, and I am somewhere in between." My lament is that both of my parents have gone, and I am somewhat farther along than somewhere in between.

ONE MIGHT WONDER if I get lonely these days at home alone. I am not feeling lonely, even with much of my time being spent alone. Perhaps I am now beyond loneliness. Several reasons for being beyond loneliness: (1) a sense of connection to the larger world; (2) thankfulness for being alive; (3) knowing that Solveig will return at the end of the day; (4) years of learning to be alone; (5) knowing that I am an integral part of my family — past, present, and future; and (6) writing in my journal, which keeps me from feeling lonely.

I identify with the unnamed protagonist of Gao Xingjian's novel *Soul Mountain.* Using the range of pronouns — I, he, you — the author (certainly the protagonist) opens a chapter with lines on the importance of being able to talk to oneself.

> You know that I am just talking to myself to alleviate my loneliness. You know that this loneliness of mine is incurable, that no-one can save me and that I can only talk with myself as the partner of my conversation.

I too write in conversation with myself. How could I be lonely?

I HAVE HAD MY ANTIBIOTIC PRESCRIPTION changed to one that will tolerate a bottle of beer. What

would a day be without a noontime visit to the Twins
Tavern?

From the rear parking lot, one walks up the steps to the
tavern. Tables and booths are filled with lunchtime cus-
tomers. I seat myself on one of the tall chairs at the bar that
runs the length of the room. The familiar sign over the bar
sends a greeting—"Beer: So Much More Than A Breakfast
Drink." Before me are the ornate handles for the pouring
of draft beer. "New Glarus Spotted Cow" is the latest addition to the selections. Packages of potato chips and salted
nuts line the counter. Knickknacks, memorabilia, bottles of
liquor, and antique fishing tackle are displayed on the back
wall. The news from WGN is on the television sets at each
end of the bar. Colored neon lights surround the room.
This is a great good place on a winter's day. A warm glow
fills the darkened space.

AT THE END OF THE DAY, Solveig will bring home
the printout of messages delivered on the Listserv for CLL.
As a subscriber, I follow the progress of fellow sufferers.
Occasionally, I contribute a message that may be of help
to others. A community, of sorts, is created—and there is
comfort in the daily reminders that we are not alone in the
disease.

A fellow subscriber raised an issue that received much
response. She wrote: "I have been playing with the thought

of not having a transplant done at all. I know it's my choice
and of course nobody is encouraging me to not have it,
but I'm seriously thinking of just making the most of my
time left, move to the beach and have quality of life there
until it's over." The evidence is far from certain on whether
treatment of any kind changes the prognosis for the disease. Statistics are presented on longevity being the same
for those treated and those not treated. We tend to think
that these overall statistics do not apply to our individual
cases.

Another subscriber reminds us this week of a sociological
survey of people over eighty years of age. They were asked
what they would do if they had their lives to live over again.
They said three things: (1) they would risk more; (2) they
would reflect more; and (3) they would do more that would
carry on after they are gone. A list that any of us, with benefit of imminent demise, could wisely contemplate.

To FLORIDA — for sunshine and a walk on the beach. A
release from this cold winter that has kept me indoors too
much of the time. To the north, the farm — my life-long
farm — is a temporary place, however much I know it and
love it. I like the line from Willa Cather that is used as an
epigraph in Edwin Way Teale's book of journal entries from
his beloved home in the woods.

We come and go but the land is always here and
the people who love and understand it are the
people to whom it belongs for a little while.

Yes, and yet: Such stock we give to place, knowing that
ultimately there is no place for us in the world. No place
that is forever ours.

March

A TWO-HOUR FLIGHT to Tampa yesterday. We flew away from a morning temperature of seven degrees in DeKalb to an afternoon temperature of eighty degrees when we landed in Florida.

The first of March, the day my mother would tell me that in other times the county roads would be traveled by wagons piled high with furniture and household belongings as tenant farmers and their families moved to the new place. It seemed that the first day of March, the day of moving, would always be stormy and that the roads would be filled with snow. Today, in Florida, we walked the beaches along the Gulf of Mexico. The sun glistened on the water's surface, shore birds ran ahead of us, and we gathered rocks and shells from the sand.

THE MESSAGE ON THE BOARD in front of the country church east of Tampa: "God's Promises Have No Expiration Date." Pawn shops line the streets leading out of town, calling for "Guns and Gold." We walk the causeway to Honeymoon Island. Quite by chance, while stopping briefly at the Moffitt Cancer Center, I meet the physician in charge of CLL patients. We stand in the lobby at the information desk reciting blood counts, and he tells me that I am doing fine. We will spend the day tomorrow with a realtor, investigating the possibilities of a part-time life near the Gulf of Mexico.

HOME AGAIN. A day of rest after yesterday's travel and the week of exploring the territories of Tampa and Sarasota. I am listening to Frederick Delius's impressionistic "Florida Suite." Memories of wide-footed cypress trees emerging from nutrient-rich dark waters, of the buildings designed by Frank Lloyd Wright on the campus of Florida Southern University, and of hiking trails at Hillsborough State Park. Today there are phone calls to respond to and e-mail messages to answer. And at noontime, I will visit the Twins Tavern just to know that I am home again.

WE ARE AT THE FARM for the weekend. Tomorrow will be the one-hundred-and-first anniversary of my father's birth. He was born on the eleventh of March, 1900, and I have always been able to know his age by the year of the century. He died in 1969, the sixty-ninth year of his life.

That would be the year I was turning thirty-five. I was

too young then to be giving him the respect he deserved.
My grieving continues out of the impossibility of ever being
able to tell him how much I love him — and how much
I respect and honor him. I keep repeating the message to
myself — daily.

My father knew I was not born for a life on the farm.
He never suggested that I might continue in his path to be
a farmer. Perhaps he thought that I might pursue the life
that he had dreams of. The irony is that no matter how
much — and how far — I have removed myself from the
farm, I return repeatedly out of great need. To know my
father — to know myself. To respect us both.

LAST NIGHT, after our supper, I stood on the back porch
of the farmhouse looking out the window into the dark
night. The light on the corner of the barn cut through the
darkness and cast shadows over the yard and along the sides
of the outbuildings. Here and there, piles of packed snow
remained. A gentle rain began to fall.

I know that no matter how much I might try to bring
a life back to the farm, the life I once knew here can never
be restored. What is gone is gone forever. The yard beyond
the house seems empty and devoid of life. Except for the
lone opossum that crawls through the crack of the barn
door escaping the cold rain. During the night, while we are
sleeping, a dusting of snow will cover the land.

This morning, after breakfast, we walked down to the
woods and around the edge of the marsh. Two Sandhill
cranes foraged and frolicked in the north field. Red-winged
blackbirds, staking out their territories, made chek-chek-
chek sounds from the tops of cattails. Three deer walked
along the ridge above the marsh. A red-tailed hawk soared
over the woods. Later in the day, we would make our way
back to Illinois.

THE IDES OF MARCH, a day we always remember on the
fifteenth of this month. It is the day that Julius Caesar was
assassinated in 44 BC by a group led by Cassius and Brutus.
Perhaps the day is a warning to us that even murder will not
restore a republic. But more likely our interest is less political, and is more an homage to William Shakespeare. I wait
this day for the results from the lab test and CT scan.

THE COPY-EDITED MANUSCRIPT for my next book
has arrived and I am reading the manuscript and answering
the queries. Fortunate, I am, to have such personal writing — my interior monologue — about to be published.

Telephone calls just received from the clinics at the
University of Wisconsin Hospital have informed me that I
have passed the lab test and the CT scan. This day — "beware
the ides of March" — has been good to me.

WELCOME, DEAR SPRING. You arrived this morning
shortly after eight. Just as I too was rising. Your rays of sun
this day will be more direct, and the earth will absorb your
energy, hungry for your offering. Still we must be patient,
as the paper reports this morning: "For several more weeks,
the chill of the past season will linger aloft, allowing more
bouts with wintry weather."

Last Sunday afternoon, in need of an outing, we drove
to the Oak Brook shopping center and walked through the
outdoor mall. And to add to the afternoon of strolling, I
purchased a fine pair of leather walking shoes.

The afternoon of walking and shopping was capped by a
spontaneous visit to Tiffany's. The shop caught our attention when we observed a large number of people gathered
inside. As soon as we entered the store, we were offered
exquisite hors d'oeuvres, desserts, and drinks. A harp-
ist played in the far corner of the room, and two beautiful women in bridal gowns meandered among the invited
guests. I overheard a professional photographer talking
about her techniques and her rates. Armed guards stood at
either side of the door. I phoned the store this morning to
find out what Tiffany's called the event we had happened
upon. We had crashed, as it turned out, a "bridal event."

On the drive home on Interstate 88, as the sun was
falling in the sky, Solveig and I listened to a tape of Alec
Guinness reading from his diary *My Name Escapes Me.*
I had read the book when it was published five years ago.

Now the pleasure of hearing his voice as he reads a March entry for the year 1996. "After dinner we discussed the idea of Scrabble or me reading some aloud (possibly Eliot's The Family Reunion) but decided bed was best." I hope that he had the chance to record from his follow-up book *A Positively Final Appearance* before he died.

FEELING A BIT DIZZY mid-morning, I went upstairs and lay down on the bed. I turned on the radio, fortunately, and listened to an interview with the Irish writer John Banville. He was on a book tour for his new novel *Eclipse,* a novel about an aging actor losing his ability to act. Banville told the interviewer that for the protagonist, as well as for himself, the world — this cosmic world — is too large. We have no discernable place in the universe.

As artists, Banville noted, and as aging actors, this world becomes even more ambiguous and uncertain to us. Such existential realization is, in fact, a source of our art, the substance of our art. There is much to know — to ponder — about chaos and the obliqueness of reality.

I will go out now and try walking along the river to the lagoon, with hopes of clearing my head. I hear wild geese flying north high over the house.

I AM LISTENING this afternoon to the cowboy singer, former rodeo rider Chris LeDoux. I bought the CD especially to hear him sing "Song of Wyoming." He sings, "I'm weary and tired, I've done my day's ridin'." Much of my inspiration in writing comes from listening to cowboy and country songs. The voices of Willie Nelson and Merle Haggard often go round in my brain as I sit at my desk and write. Songs of the highway, of leaving home, of missing the ones you love make up my repertoire—along with the classical nocturnes of Chopin and the requiems of Fauré, Brahms, and Mozart. Sounds and sensibilities for a lifetime.

Happily I report that my uroflow test flowed nicely this morning, and that the results of my PSA test were satisfactory. Earlier this week, my dermatologist told me that the basal cell carcinoma that he had removed from my leg has healed. I am in good shape, apparently, for another six months, according to both dermatologist and urologist.

SUNDAY WAS A DAY of cultural riches, popular and classical. A day of the spirit's moving, as the day can sometimes be. The Academy Awards were presented in the evening as Solveig and I propped ourselves up on the basement bed and marked our ballots. The highlight of the evening for us—and for much of the audience in Hollywood—was Bob Dylan singing his song "Things Have Changed."

Following the performance, which was telecast live from Australia, the award for best original song was presented to Dylan. Caught by surprise, his acceptance was gracious and offered with good wishes.

Early in the afternoon we had driven to the movie theater in Geneva to see the Coen brothers' "O Brother, Where Art Thou?" About the Depression—about living in the Depression with the help of music. The movie's screenplay, adapted from Homer's *Odyssey,* is about wanderers, as we all are, on the run. That we—you and I—might be like the Hellenic heroes, inspiration for other generations. Thus we tell our daily and most intimate tales.

This morning, not having Bob Dylan's new song on CD, I am playing a song he recorded in 1971, "I Shall Be Released." I see my reflection, a life shining. Any day now. Any day now.

WHILE I REWIND another movie video, Solveig offers the comment, "Maybe we have watched enough movies for a while." So much depends upon the movies in our times. Movies are a spiritual source, a validation of our contemporary existence, another way of telling the story. As a rest from the movies, I will drive to the bookstore and buy a copy of the newest translation of the *Odyssey,* returning the video "Almost Famous" on the way to the store. With

warmer weather coming in another month, there will be
things to do beyond movies and books.

ONE LINE from Charles Wright's poem "March Journal"
will suffice:

> Buds hold their breaths and sit tight.

April

OLD SNOW IS PILED in the ditches and on the north sides of hills as we drive to the farm. It is a bright Sunday morning, in spite of yesterday's forecast of snow and sleet. Having borrowed a pickup truck, we are taking a sofa up to the farm to replace the one that has served the house for forty years. Neighbors meet us in the driveway and help us carry the sofa through the front porch door into the living room. A cold wind blows all over the farm. We forego a walk to the woods and marsh, and sleepily drive back to DeKalb.

WAITING FOR THE FIRST THUNDERSTORM of the season. While waiting, I listen to the songs from the movie "Wonder Boys." The songs of self-revelation written over the last fifty years by songwriters in search of meaning and redemption. I play over again John Lennon's line on missing the big time, on wondering about no longer being "on the ball." Bob Dylan sings about the day not being dark yet, "but it's getting there." Then I put on a CD by Lou Donaldson and listen to his song "Just a Dream (on My Mind)." He sings about waking up in the morning, after a

night of dreaming, and not a thing could he find. His alto
saxophone solo blends with Lonnie Smith's organ riffs.

To gain contact with my own reality, I will walk downtown in the soft, gray morning light. I will stroll along
Lincoln Highway once again, the street that runs from one
coast of the country to the other. And I will know that I am
someplace between one shore and another.

A MANUSCRIPT HAS ARRIVED in the morning mail
for my review. Another accounting, a memoir beauti-
fully researched and written, of the generations of another
Wisconsin family. I will do all I can to ensure its publication.

The author wonders provocatively how there can be patterns of the past without a pattern-maker. Yet patterns there
are. Perhaps we who remember and reconstruct are the pattern-
makers. We are the ultimate pattern-makers who give order
to the lives that have gone before us. Likely there will be
others who will eventually come to find the order in our lives.

THE BLUETS are dotting the lawns in town. Clusters of
daffodils have started to bloom this afternoon in the front
yard. A warm wind blows all day long. After yesterday's
thunderstorm, green grass is beginning to appear from
under winter's musty mats of brown. The golf course at the
country club has turned completely green.

I must prepare the report on my reading of the memoir. I am reminded in the memoir, as well as in my own writing, that when a writer appears in the family, the family is forever changed. We alter a phenomenon by our act of observation. In writing about one's family, in making one's own interpretation, the family is certain to be altered. Writers pass to others their stories, their constructions of reality. One must take great care in the stories that are told.

EARLY ON A MORNING sixty-one years ago today, Germany began its occupation of Norway. Troops marched into the cities along the coast. By evening, the country was secured, except for continuing resistance in the snowy north. As citizens of Stavanger were fleeing to the countryside for fear of being bombed, Solveig's mother called the midwife, and Solveig was born. Last night, with Solveig's children and grandchildren, we celebrated her birthday. Freshly picked daffodils decorated the table. Among my simple greetings was a new gathering of writings by Mark Twain, titled *The Diary of Adam and Eve.* The children danced to songs of Bob Dylan.

A night of rain drove the fertilizer into the lawn. April showers are bringing April flowers. This noon we leave for Madison for a needed examination at the hospital.

MY BROTHER RALPH and I met at the farm to make
plans for spring planting. We sat around the kitchen table
talking to the District Conservationist representing the U.S.
Department of Agriculture, and to the Wildlife Biologist
from the Wisconsin Department of Natural Resources. In
a few weeks we will be planting trees and prairie grasses
under the Conservation Reserve Program. Soon the old
grasses — primarily reed canary — will be burned around
the pond at the old place. Eventually the ecosystem around
the pond will be restored and will provide a rejuvenated
brooding habitat for water birds. Someday — years from
now — the black oaks and white oaks and burr oaks that we
are planting will give shelter and sustenance to other life.

Driving to the farm, I heard Garrison Keillor announce
that the writer Glenway Wescott was born in Wisconsin
one hundred years ago. For a very short time Wescott was
a Wisconsin writer, before leaving Wisconsin in his early
twenties for Europe, and eventually settling into a literary
life on the East Coast. In 1928 he published his book *Good-
Bye Wisconsin.* He wrote in the title story of the book:
"How much sweeter to come and go than to stay; that by
way of judgment upon Wisconsin." In the same going-away
story, he wrote, "The Middle West is nowhere; an abstract
nowhere." Wescott has his young character wishing at the
end of the story for the disappearance within himself of his
origins and his prejudices and his Wisconsin.

A long time ago, I left Wisconsin with similar thoughts

and desires and expectations for a life in a larger world. Here I am back on the land that once was my home, and from which I sought to escape. And here I am now trying to preserve and protect that land. But happy, at the same time, that I have had life elsewhere.

WE HAVE JUST RETURNED from Madison again for what I thought would be a routine appointment with my hematologist. He walked into the office, where we were waiting after the nurse had checked my vital signs, and asked me if he had ever mentioned the removal of my spleen. I said that the subject had come up during my first visit to his office. The problem is that my white blood counts are low — again — with neutrophils down to 500. Tomorrow morning I will begin the four infusions of Rituxan that will be given once each week. Hopefully, the disease will be controlled and the counts will improve. With low counts, there is the danger of infection. I wonder and worry about the invasion of the aspergillus fungus that comes with spring and is stirred by the winds that blow over these Midwestern fields.

THIS EASTER DAY I read some of the letters that members of my family have sent to each other over the last fifty years. Perhaps some of the sadness — and the melancholy—that has accumulated during the last week will be relieved by reading and remembering. All the words we have given to each other—in letters to and from father, mother, brother, grandparents, daughters, nieces and nephew, uncle and aunt, and cousins. Letters that I keep on the high shelf of my closet.

News of the risen Christ brings little hope to me this Easter Day. Only the love, the reminder of love, in these letters offers hope to me.

A card from my mother two Easters ago, two weeks before she died, wishes us Easter joy and happiness. She adds, "Thank you for all the things you have done for me." She sends her love. On this day, exactly two years ago, my mother passed away as I held her hand in mine.

THE LETTERS always send news about the weather. My mother and father wrote to me upon their return to the farm after visiting me in New York, and after thankful expressions they described the weather back home. Whenever I would write home, I would not fail to mention the weather, wherever I was living or traveling. And so it went on for years—news of the weather exchanged in letters. It is weather that holds us together.

This afternoon's weather has turned dark and cold, and snow is beginning to fall. I have decided to watch Claude Lelouch's 1966 romantic film "A Man and a Woman."

A lyric near the end of the movie informs me: "Though
we go on pretending, we cannot change the ending."
Weatherwise, outside my window, the snow has stopped
falling—leaving no trace—and the sun is shining late this
afternoon.

I HAVE FOUND THE LETTER written home in the fall
of 1956. I found it recently in the top drawer of the desk
on the farm. In the letter I am telling my father and mother
about my first experience of teaching. I had been sent by
Kimball Young, my graduate adviser, to the Chicago campus
of Northwestern University to administer an examination
to his sociology class. My assignment also was to deliver a
ten-minute lecture—my first ever—to a class of students
I would find seated in a large auditorium. Later in the evening, after returning to my room at the Evanston campus, I
wrote to my parents that I had made the long walk up to the
lecture table without falling. I ended my letter, "The evening
is over and I feel that at last there is something I can do."
For the next thirty-two years I would do what I had found I
could do. And the letters continued to be written until there
was no longer any reason to keep writing home.

MY DAUGHTER ANNE, visiting from her home and work
in Oxford, Mississippi, helped me drive to Madison last

Friday. Midway through the Rituxan treatment, the nurse brought us the good news that my neutrophils had risen to 2500 since the treatment of a week ago. We celebrated over an early dinner at a Turkish restaurant on Monroe Street.

The CD we had brought along for listening during the ride was of blues music from the South. The writer of the liner notes points out that "blues is about the fluctuations on our emotional stock exchange, the everyday gains and losses of the spirit." The music is about "keeping your options open." We listened to Memphis Minnie, Robert Johnson, Brownie McGhee, Bessie Smith, Blind Boy Fuller, and Stevie Ray Vaughan as the eighteen-wheelers passed us left and right on Interstate 90.

ALL NIGHT LONG the northwest wind blew against the windows and sent rattling sounds throughout the house. Dreams forgotten in the morning ebbed and flowed during the night. The comforter was repeatedly thrown off and pulled up again.

This morning I am listening to Leopold Stokowski's recording of the Cinderella ballet by Sergei Prokofiev. I am listening to it because of a conversation that Anne and I had about her interest in deciphering the meanings of things — cultural, social, and personal. Behind our stories — especially the stories we read to our children — are levels of meaning below the surface.

Anne's university students in the French class that she
teaches are reading "Cendrillon" and "Le Petit Chaperon
Rouge." Behind each story is a kind of violence, a cruelty,
a dark side that we leave the young to ponder. In the one
story Cinderella is ill-treated at home and in the other story
Little Red Riding Hood is deceived by a devouring wolf.
One must beware of appearances.

We discuss the matter of appearances and the search for
a deeper meaning, and the likelihood that the superficial is
deceptive. Freud and Marx and Darwin continue to lead
us to the underlying meaning of things. I tell Anne that as
I get older I tend to find enough mystery in the everyday
world of appearance. Lately I prefer the surface, satisfied
with the life that is presented to me at the moment. We
laugh—my daughter and I—at the pleasure of such talk.
Both of us realize that these thoughts are spiritual commu-
nications as we travel the interstate on our way home.

POEMS WRITTEN ON SUNDAY MORNINGS by Wendell
Berry are the poems my mother gave to me three years ago
on my birthday. In an inscription, she wished me "many
more happy years." This day of April, in 1906, my mother
was born. I celebrate and remember her life this Sabbath
morning.

In a Sabbath poem written a year after his mother's
death, Wendell Berry listens to the happy, sweet notes of

the redbird, and he grieves his mother's leaving of "this world forever." I remember a spring morning, when I was very young, gathering wildflowers on a sunny hill and in a woodland — violets, buttercups, and a shooting star — and carrying them home to my mother on her birthday. This year's April is about to end.

May

THIS IS A DAY of primordial significance, a day of transition and transformation. The ancient Romans gave thanks on this day to Flora, the flower goddess. The Celts built bonfires to ward off evil spirits. In Medieval England, villagers went "a-maying," dancing around a maypole and paying homage to a local Queen. Each May as I was growing up on the farm, my cousin Gail would walk across the field and leave a May basket at my door. And on the first of May in 1959, my daughter Laura was born.

THE NEW YORK TIMES reports this morning—on the weather page—that during the next few weeks "much of the nation will complete the transition from the capricious nature of early spring to the reliable warmth of summer." Rising heat and humidity of May will bring an increase in the number of severe storms in the Midwest. The weather channel is already predicting intermittent storms for the weekend. We plan to be at the farm following Friday's Rituxan treatment in Madison.

THE SWEET BIRDS have returned to the farm for another season. I have assisted their return and reproduction by nailing a bluebird house to the fence post and hanging a wren house on a limb of the lilac bush. Upon the boughs this season, birds will sing their songs. Already, from the kitchen window, I watch as twigs are being brought to the nest.

The planting of four hundred oaks on the hills rising east of the pond has brought us together for another day at the farm. Seedlings no more than three inches tall are being put into the ground. Someday, a hundred years from now, others will walk in woods and observe the accomplishments of the trees. The trees that will stand, and in the night, as Paul Zimmer writes in his poem " Final Affection," will prop "darkness up to the silence."

My brother and I find time to make a few repairs on the barn and on the sheds that are losing their sidings and their window panes. Defying the season of renewal and new beginnings, rot steadily makes its way. We sit at the kitchen table and find comfort in talk. A blessing, it is, to know and to experience the seasons of life.

ON THE FLOOR of the attic of the farmhouse, in a broken cardboard box, I have found a few trinkets and artifacts rescued from the old house when it was torn down in 1942. Among the items is the black-glass rosary that probably belonged to my father's aunt Kate. A gray clay pipe rests in the bottom of the box, the pipe that I had seen my great-grandmother Bridget holding in a photograph. I was told by my father that she brought the pipe with her from Ireland and smoked it regularly. More of the past can be found in the box when I am of a disposition to look.

YESTERDAY while watching the old movie "Grapes of Wrath," I heard the preacher — the one who once was a preacher in Oklahoma — offer these words at the brief funeral of Grandfather Joad: "I heard a fellow say a poem once, and he said, 'all that lives is holy'." And in the parking lot of the supermarket later in the day, I saw a bumper sticker which proclaimed that God is watching over us whether we know it or not. There is no place, no person or thing of existence that is outside the realm of the sacred. Why I am interested in this fact today, I do not know.

I HAVE COMPLETED reading Richard Bernstein's new book *Ultimate Journey*. The Buddhist monk Hsuan Tsang began his journey in the year 629, and returned home to China sixteen years later. Even in the early time, ruins marked his path. I like Bernstein's observation:

> Both of us, I would think, experienced a certain rev-
> erence for ruins as dignified emblems of the eternal
> human condition. They are humbling, these piles of
> stone, because they attest at once to the imperma-
> nence of things and to the grand temerity involved in
> the effort to make them permanent.

The lesson about the ruins is timeless, learned and relearned
each generation. Bernstein concludes his meditation on
ruins by noting, "The past is a great teacher, and I was im-
pressed that in the case of this particular past, the seventh-
century monk from China and I would be confronted with
the same lessons."

As the leaves fill out the trees, and as the grasses grow
high, it is time to consider the truth of ruins. Soon I can
begin to photograph the things that have come to ruin
in my own lifetime. A summer's journey that will lead to
autumn and to the wintering of the places close to home.

APPARENTLY I NEED to spend more time at the farm.
Not the farm itself, perhaps, but a place where I can
gather myself anew. I am feeling like the character I have
been reading about in Larry McMurtry's novel *Duane's
Depressed.* One day Duane stops driving his pickup truck,
parks it forever, and begins walking. He walks down the
dirt road to his cabin in the country. McMurtry writes: "He

wanted to hang on to the new, uplifting feeling of possibility that he had felt when he first stepped out of his house: the feeling that he had a new life to live, a life of walking, of unburdened solitude, or a different way of looking at the world." For me, this is a time—even in the midst of uncertain prognosis—to be born again.

WHAT YOU ARE LOOKING FOR is already within yourself. I was reminded of this while a friend visited me last week on his way from Indiana to Iowa. Wanting to show Hal the place that appears in most of my writings, we drove up to the farm for a day. This is the place that I have spent a lifetime looking for—the place that was near all the time.

I am at the farm again, having driven up yesterday with the intent of photographing the farm buildings. The light is not right for the photographs that I want to take, so I am working on a number of chores. While gathering wild asparagus along the road for last night's supper, I stood motionless and watched a fox run across the tilled land east of the barn. A weasel scurried into the ditch. A marsh harrier, in sleek silhouette, glided over the stubbled field. Thrushes and thrashers were feeding under the brush at the aging orchard. The invading honeysuckle bloomed profusely along the roadside. I slept soundly throughout the night in the farmhouse. In the morning, goldfinches gathered for thistle seed at the feeder beyond the kitchen window. This place — whether I am far or near — continues to be the center of my life.

It is my birthday today. Sixty-seven and pleased to be here. As is my habit on the day of my birth, I will walk the streets and byways of this prairie town. I am happily honored with gifts of books.

A bright day with a clear sky. I have planted a bush tomato in front of the house, and one in a pot on the back patio. Song birds are conspicuously absent this week; the feeders remain filled and unattended. Occasionally a cardinal or a blue jay flies through the yard. Perhaps the wandering neighborhood cat has made the song birds find other places to feed and nest.

Up and by car to the farm. A humid and overcast day. I have peonies to plant at the cemetery. Monday morning we will drive from the farm to Madison for an appointment with my doctor.

We performed a number of chores at the farm this afternoon and evening: replacing the mailbox blown down by the wind, planting tomatoes on the south side of the chicken house, filling the birdfeeders, watering the maple

planted last week at the entrance to the driveway, and pick-
ing asparagus for supper. The chorus frogs sing their songs
from the pond down at the old place.

MY NEUTROPHILS are dropping in numbers, but are still
at the good level of 2000. I learned from my doctor what I
have been denying all along—that the Rituxan treatments
provide only temporary relief from the disease. It is our
hope that repeated infusions will continue to restore my
neutrophils. The chronic problem is the failure of neutrophils to develop in my bone marrow. Someday—in two or
three years perhaps—other drugs may be available for our
experimentation. In the meantime, regulation of dosage is
the course of action.

I DROVE THE BACKROADS listening to the soundtrack
of the French film "The Umbrellas of Cherbourg." Earlier
in the week I had watched the movie twice on a rented
video. I also watched the French film "A Heart in Winter."
The third time I have watched this movie. Both films deal
with matters of the heart. With some sorrow, I had to
decline an invitation to visit Paris this summer, in deference
to my neutrophils. The heart is heavy and my white cells
are in jeopardy.

I PLANTED BRIGHT RED PEONIES at the graves of
John and Bridget Quinney, my great-grandparents. To
commemorate their lives, to recognize their courage in leaving Ireland during the potato famine and crossing the ocean
to begin lives in a new and foreign place. The decision to
emigrate was relatively easy, given the alternatives of unem-
ployment and starvation in County Kilkenny in the 1840s.
Each spring red peonies will mark John and Bridget's
earthly destinies. I can only imagine their lives, but I am
here before their graves by grace of their having lived.

THE DAY BEFORE MEMORIAL DAY, and we have spotted the wild turkey stalking the tilled field and vanishing
into tall grass. On our long walk to the pond, we picked
asparagus still growing along the fence line and the old road
at the bottom of the hill.

My reading this weekend is Larry McMurtry's new book
Paradise. He is on a cargo ship making stops at the islands
of the Marquesas in the Pacific, and he is thinking about his
father and mother's travels, and their lack of travels, and the
approaching last days of his mother's life. His mother and
father had a long marriage that ended in separation. They
were happy in their innocence for a while on the plains of
Texas. But then, as McMurtry writes, "life turned from
under them like a fine cutting horse will turn out from
under an inexperienced rider."

I pay close attention to McMurtry's observation on the sadness that he is feeling aboard ship. He thinks that he may be "suffering a kind of metaphysical diminishment, in relation to the vastness, the majesty, and the eternity of the sea." The way I may be feeling as I walk the fields and woods and marshes on the farm. And McMurtry's sadness may also be a feeling of "marginality" coming from his last bout with a life-threatening illness and surgery. Yet, he has come on a long voyage to sense farness, to sense, perhaps, "the possibility of one's nonexistence." Traveling in vast spaces, the possibility of nonexistence is hard to avoid.

MEMORIAL DAY, and we have driven the five miles to Delavan to see if the day is being observed in town. Yes, after one hundred and thirty years, the war dead are still being remembered with a parade through town and a memorial service on the hill in Spring Grove Cemetery. We follow the procession to the cemetery. Not since 1952, when I played in the high school band for the last time, had I been a part of this procession.

We are surrounded by headstones and by the tall ever-greens reaching into the sky. There are prayers, and speeches, and the honoring of the last living Gold Star mother. The band plays somber numbers and the youth choir sings "America the Beautiful." War veterans, some in their original uniforms from the various wars, form two lines in front of the Civil War monument. Finally, five representatives of the branches of the military advance to the monument and upon command fire three volleys of shots into the air. Babies in the crowd cry from the sudden, loud firing of the guns, a release of sorts. The morning is beautiful, and we all slowly prepare to take our leave of the cemetery. I briefly walk the grounds to check on the progress of the peonies that I have planted at the family graves. I thank the minister for offering the morning prayer.

MY LITTLE GRANDSON JULIAN celebrates his first birthday. He is far away, already, traveling with his parents and brother to Nicosia and London. We were in London renting a flat in Chelsea last year when I received the call from Laura that Julian had been born earlier that day in Boston. He will be a traveler all his life, in the family tradition, I am certain.

THE MONTH OF MAY COMES TO AN END. The sweet birds now sing in the trees in town and on the farm. Soon the days of summer. A time to make hay. Remembering Maxwell Anderson's cautionary lyrics to Kurt Weill's "September Song."

Oh, it's a long, long while
From May to December,
But the days grow short,
When you reach September.

These few precious days I'll spend with you.

June

LET JUNE BEGIN with an early morning welcome. May I be like the son of Odysseus, rising to Dawn's rose-red fingers, in Homer's *Odyssey*.

> When young Dawn with her rose-red fingers shone
>   once more
> the true son of Odysseus sprang from bed and
>   dressed,
> over his shoulder he slung his well-honed sword,
> fastened rawhide sandals under his smooth feet
> and stepped from his bedroom, handsome as a god.

For weeks I have been reading Homer's classic tale, and listening in the car to the tapes of the words spoken elegantly by Ian McKellen. I envision myself on the wine-dark sea as I cross the prairie. And on some mornings, I think of myself rising handsome as a god.

COOL DAYS and unsettled weather. Thunderstorms and sharp lightning in the night. I take my afternoon naps daily without fail. A sound sleep sets me right for the rest of the day. A relief, today, from the report in the science section of the newspaper which says that the universe encompasses all possibilities until it is observed to have a particular set of physical rules. Everything exists everywhere at once until we make our human observations. We are the creators of the universe. In the meantime, I celebrate today the birth of my brother, born sixty-five years ago.

WE SPEND A LIFETIME — in all of our labors and entertainments — trying to avoid the fact of our ultimate earthly end. I am fairly successful in not thinking constantly the thought. Except on gray days and during rainy spells that last the week. There are promises of sunshine for the weekend.

All the while, astronomers keep peering into space for distant objects up to three billion light years away. The science report for today: "These are quasars, young galaxies with supermassive black holes so powerful that they consume surrounding matter in prodigious gulps, generating energies that send beacons of light shining across the universe." Light from distant quasars has been observed, "emitted when the universe was less than 800 million years old and 7.2 times smaller than it is today." All of this is seen from the vantage point of a small planet we call Earth.

Also in the morning paper is the obituary of the musician

John Hartford. He played stringed instruments and wrote one of country music's most recorded songs, "Gentle on My Mind." When he learned several years ago that death was approaching, because of cancer, he became obsessed with practicing the fiddle. He worked to become as good a craftsman as possible in the time he had left. Staving off the ultimate end as best he could.

DAWN'S LOVELY LOCKS stream through the layers of fog as I stand early this morning looking over the fields to the hills east of the barn. Later in the morning a crew of archaeologists will arrive from the University of Wisconsin in Milwaukee to make systematic probes into the oak knoll that rises from the marsh. The hope is to document the occupation of the land around the marsh by the Potawatomi before European settlement. My great-grandmother Bridget told my father of seeing the Potawatomi returning to the place where they had once lived. Others reported that burial sites had been found. This day's work will not confirm these stories, but the archaeologists will return another day to continue their search using other methods and equipment. They will also begin to document the settlement of the farm by generations of my family. It is my wish that these acres will someday become a public preserve for others to enjoy and appreciate. We are becoming the old ones who once lived on this land.

MY BROTHER AND I survey the condition of the barn and
surrounding buildings. The wooden chicken house — the
long and low building that runs east and west to the north
of the barn — is rotting rapidly and is beyond repair. We
will let the chicken house make its own way to oblivion.
It will be a ruin that will be a reminder of a life once lived
here. Earlier in the week — while browsing in a bookstore
in Milwaukee — I found these lines in a recent poem by
Robert Bly:

> The Harvesters will come in at the end of time
> And tell us that the crop of ruin has been great.

THE DEER TICK crawls around the inside of the fruit jar.
It has been to the DeKalb Clinic with me this afternoon
for identification. I found the tick this morning burrowing
into my leg as I was taking a bath. I assume that it had been
resting in the clothes that I had worn last Saturday when I
went with the archaeologists to the oak knoll in search of
Potawatomi burials. Because of my compromised immune
system, the doctor is treating me as if I have Lyme disease.
Antibiotics have been prescribed for the week, and I am to
watch for a rash and swelling. Another danger — the bites
of disease-carrying insects — that goes with farming, and
with my search for the past.

DAWN, goddess of the morning, with her rose-red fingers rises once more east of the barn and lights the morning sky. I have taken the folding chair to sit behind the barn and watch the sun rise and listen to the early morning sounds. Barn swallows swoop around me. The great blue heron flies gracefully out of the tamaracks at the edge of the marsh. Song birds are awakening in the trees surrounding the house. The Baltimore oriole emerges from its basket-nest in the Chinese elm. I hear pheasants calling and cackling from the far end of the field across the road. The two Sandhill cranes are pulling sprouted corn from the planted rows and are sending deep-throated rattles into the morning air. The crescent moon with bright Venus to its left hangs in the eastern sky above the old and empty corncrib. To my back, red Mars is sinking below the western horizon.

A morning for Odysseus to behold. He would be on his homeward journey — in Book Nine of Homer's *Odyssey* — and about to meet the Lotus-eaters and then sail on to the shores of the Cyclopes. Odysseus pauses to think about his home in Ithaca, no sweeter sight on earth:

> So nothing is as sweet as a man's own country,
> his own parents, even though he's settled down
> in some luxurious house, off in a foreign land
> and far from those who bore him.

Such a place — my own native country — spreads before me this morning on a day in the middle of June.

THE SUMMER SOLSTICE occurred early this morning when the sun reached its highest point above the earth's equator. The weather section of the morning paper describes the astronomical event, saying that summer officially begins this day in the United States when the noontime sun is directly overhead at the Tropic of Cancer, 23.5 degrees of latitude north of the equator. For the ease of record keeping, climatologists consider summer to be the months of June, July, and August.

At any rate, this will be the longest day of the year here in the northern hemisphere. And this is the first summer solstice of the new millennium. For many people on this planet, the day marks mid-summer, rather than the first day of summer. In this country, however, we think that summer cannot begin until the occurrence of the solstice. Perhaps we have wanted to savor the spring, or maybe we have preferred the thought of a summer yet to come.

What I know for certain this day, this year, is that my absolute neutrophil count is at a high of 3500. My doctor is surprised, and we all are pleased. The solstice is predictable, and my neutrophils are a mystery. Let the summer begin.

A ROAD TRIP over the weekend to Michigan to celebrate the marriage of Karen and Paul. In the evening, Solveig and I drove the few miles into East Lansing and with good fortune came upon a summer solstice jazz festival being held out-of-doors at the Ann Street Plaza near the campus of Michigan State University. A jazz quartet, with a guest trumpeter from Detroit, played into the night. The evening ended with a joyous rendition of "When the Saints Go Marching In." The next morning, after locating the state capitol building, we made our way home. Along the highway a large billboard proclaimed, "I don't question your existence—God." The Sunday afternoon traffic was heavy around Chicago.

THE PATTERN I seem to be falling into these months—naturally and with fair ease—is captured and defined in a poem I heard last week on Garrison Keillor's "The Writer's Almanac." The poem—"where we are"—is by the West Coast poet Gerald Locklin. The poem begins by stating an envy of those who live in two places. Going from one place to another allows us to transfer our unease from our own lives to matters of place. With two homes, every move is a "homecoming." The poet writes that he has

> always loved both the freshness of
> arriving and the relief of leaving.

I too — moving back and forth weekly between town and farm — keep hope alive. And so to the farm already at midweek.

WITHIN A WEEK'S TIME, summer has come to the farm. The corn grew at least eight inches during the last week of June. The sky-blue blossoms of the chicory plant, blossoms that glow in the light of day, are beginning to appear along the roadside. Large clusters of white flowers cover the elderberry bushes. Long-stalked daylilies — with their orange funnel-shaped flowers — are at road's edge. Ripe mulberries are dropping to the ground. A second cutting of alfalfa matures in the field. The brown heads of Indian grass and switch grass wave gently in the warm morning breeze.

At first light, drawing a glass of cold water from the kitchen faucet, I spot through the open window a gray fox with a bushy, white-tipped tail running across the lawn and down the fence line to the woods. This is the day that we will attempt to remove the dust and dirt from the basement floor. An overture by Aaron Copeland begins to play on the classical music station. On the front porch, I sit in the rocking chair between the trunks that came generations ago from the old country.

July

To the porch immediately upon rising. I have been curious throughout the night about the contents of the trunks. At various times over the years I have opened the trunks, investigated an item or two, and closed the lids for another day. This morning I have removed from one of the trunks a child's desk case and a wooden cigar box with the trademark label "Lucke's Little Cigars." The cigar box, which belonged to my grandfather Holloway, contains four arrowheads, a pair of seashell cuff links, assorted buttons, a glass bottle stopper, a large marble, and a few small stones.

The child's case—a six-by-ten-inch black cardboard box with the embossed letters "Writing Desk"—belonged to the sister of my mother's mother. A few belongings of Leah Taylor were placed in her school writing case when she died at the age of ten in 1888. The case contains penciled lists of school grades, colored cards of dancing children, a small roll of mending materials with thread, needle, and pins. There is an ornate metal plate engraved "Leah—Our Darling." And in the case was placed the obituary from the local newspaper. I am struck by the words on paper now yellow and brittle, and by the literary and spiritual expression of the obituary. The sentiments are likely common to the death notices of the times, but still, I am struck by the effort and devotion that goes beyond the newspaper notices of today. I will copy the words for Leah Taylor into my journal.

> —September 7, 1988, will ever remain a day of sad remembrance to the family of Mr. and Mrs. Charles Taylor, of La Grange, who, on that day was bereft of a most amiable child, whose youthful promise had given rise to an unusual degree of paternal hope and comfort. As the most beautiful flowers bloom but for an hour and then leave us to regret their brief existence, so the most promising of earth's fairest children seem to mock us with their early departure. Seldom do we meet a child of ten years in whom are combined to so remarkable a degree the various qualities that render childhood promising. Possessing as she did a most amiable disposition, talents and judgment far in advance of her years, Leah was a favorite at home and among all who knew her. Though the grief which attends the loss of one so dear cannot be consoled, it may to some extent be lightened by the sympathetic words of Robert Burns:
>
>> My child, thou art gone to the home of thy rest,
>>> Where the songs of the good,
>>> Where the hymns of the blest,

Through an endless existence shall charm thee.

The funeral ceremonies took place at the La Grange church on Sunday, Sept. 9, and were conducted by the Rev. B.T. White. The entire school of which she was a member followed in procession the remains of the one they so dearly loved to the church yard where the flowers which they carried were strewn upon the grave.

> "This early bud that's nipped so soon
>   Shall rise and bloom beyond the tomb."

Later in the morning, we drive to Round Prairie cemetery in LaGrange. I want to locate the place where more than a hundred years ago children carried flowers and strewed them upon the grave of their classmate. What remains this Sunday morning is Leah's school case with its few contents as evidence of a life. We remember. Generations later, lives are touched.

I HAVE DECIDED to stay at the farm through the weekend. Yesterday's Fourth of July passed quietly. From the porch, we watched the night sky for explosions of fireworks over Delavan. The moon was about to become full. In the sky at dawn, the planets Jupiter, Mercury, Saturn, and Venus could be seen. To our surprise, a coyote, the first I have ever seen on the farm, ran across the lawn south of the house. Solveig then started back to DeKalb for two days of work, and I went to the porch, where I noticed that a deer tick was just beginning to crawl up my arm.

Later in the day, I completed my rereading of Albert Camus's memoir, thinly disguised as a novel, *The First Man.* The manuscript for the book was found in his briefcase when he died in the auto accident in 1960. I paid attention to a note that Camus attached to the end of the manuscript. "The nobility of the writer's occupation lies in resisting oppression, thus in accepting isolation." Throughout the accounting of his early years, Camus shows the extent to which one creates a life, bound by stark necessity. Camus was prepared for "all that life has that is good, that is mysterious, that is not and never will be for sale." We all are presented with a world unknown to us, and we spend a lifetime creating ourselves within that world.

Two woodchucks stand upright looking toward the house. I stand in the shadows of the kitchen so that I will not be seen. A young woodchuck in the family peers from the hole in the granary door. The woodchucks obviously sense my presence in the house. Their curiosity is measured by the minutes they stay motionless looking in my direction. The two adults, standing tall with long teeth protruding, appear to be holding hands. They eventually resume their four-legged posture and return to the culvert under the driveway.

Evening now, after sunset, and still the wrens are singing in the trees. I wait for the full moon to rise.

CERTAINLY I AM HERE ALONE to get some idea of what living in the farmhouse was for my parents. They lived in this house from the time of their marriage in 1930, having built the house the previous year for the life they would create here together. I, too, lived here, for eighteen years, until I left for college. All around me are the signs and artifacts of the years. Although the house has been cleaned and half-heartedly rearranged since my mother died two years ago, the house is pretty much as she made it her home for the thirty years after my father died.

I will never really know what life in this house was for my mother as she lived alone. She had friends here that I do not have; she received phone calls daily from neighbors down the road and across the field; she drove to town every day—sometimes several times a day—to do her shopping and her banking and simply to go to town for the ride. My mother was a member of the Methodist church in Delavan, and was involved in several of the activities in the church, as well as regularly attending services on Sunday. She also was a volunteer until the end of her life at the nursing home in town, working every Thursday afternoon. And my mother lived with memories that are naturally different from mine. I sense in this house a presence that is other than my own.

I CANNOT BE AT THE FARM long without imagining that I am a character in Chekhov's play "Uncle Vanya."

The Russian estate on which the drama takes place belongs to the old order that is fading. I, too, am of a passing order, and I am not certain of my place in the coming order. Repairs are being made on the house; the land is rented out to pay the taxes; trees and native grasses are being planted on previously tilled land, and fields are returning to their native state. I am a caretaker with little notion of what is to come.

I reread the play today, and viewed once again Louis Malle's film "Vanya on 42nd Street," directed by André Gregory. The characters and the dialogue seem contemporary. A century apart, but in both times we are experiencing the passing of one world and the beginning of another. I identify most with the doctor, Astrov, who also plans and manages the forest. Near the beginning of the play, Astrov completes a dialogue, speaking to Marina, the old nurse: "And I thought of the men and women who will be alive a hundred or a couple hundred years after we've gone, those we're preparing the way for. Will they have a good word to say for us? You know Nanny, they won't even remember us." Nanny replies, "Man may forget, but God will remember." The doctor, letting her thought prevail, answers, "Thank you for saying that. You put it very well."

RETURNED TO THE CITY Sunday night. With more time being spent at the farm, returning to DeKalb — even with its relatively small population of thirty-some

thousand—seems to be a return to the "city." A relief, in
a way, to get away from the chores, such as they are, of the
farm. And away from the decay—the rot and the rust.

The assortment of hand-made quilts that we found in
the attic are now hanging on the line in the backyard. Some
of the quilts are more than a hundred years old. Swatches of
material in the crazy quilt are unknown to the modern eye.
Hopefully the morning breeze will remove some of the dust
from years of storage in the attic.

I found the deeds to the lands that make up the farm.
Acres of land have been acquired by generations of my
family over the last one hundred and thirty years. The first
deed is for the few acres purchased by my great-grandfather
John Quinney in 1868. Some years after fleeing the famine
in Ireland, he and Bridget settled forever in a house by the
lilac bushes, overlooking the marsh and the muskrat pond.
Beside his name on the deed is his substitute for a signa-
ture—a large X. Oh, pioneers!

I HAVE IMAGINED a project, a meditation on the passing
of time. I would return to the landscape I knew as a child.
Much of that landscape remains as a reminder of life in a
former time. In the ruins, especially in the ruins, are the
outlines of a bygone era. Out of the old order—out of the
ruins—we live our daily lives. I would see the landscape of
home from the perspective of the returning native.

Along the way, the sensibility of the project has changed. Or better, my sensibility about the homeplace is in the process of changing. True, the place—the farm—is filled with reminders of a bygone environment, of a domestic existence that no longer exists. Yet I am not trying to reenact the myth of a glorious past that has been lost. And maybe, as J. B. Jackson writes in his book *The Necessity for Ruins,* "the old farmhouse has to decay before we can restore it and lead an alternative life style in the country." But my aims are more simple and direct: I am here to know the place, perhaps to know it for the first time, and to make it a part of my life as I am living it now. The joy I have in the homeplace is heightened by, not replaced by, memory of being here in another time. I know that the only time I have is here in the present moment.

A MORNING OF LISTENING to the sounds of music. Already, and the morning is young, I have heard Merle Haggard sing "Wishing All These Old Things Were New" from his current album. I have listened carefully to Arvo Pärt's haunting "Spiegel in Spiegel." Nina Simone has been singing "Love's Been Good to Me" and "The More I See You." Right now I am listening to the songs on the album the Nitty Gritty Dirt Band released in 1972, a studio album featuring bluegrass songwriters and singers, including Doc Watson, Maybelle Carter, Merle Travis, and Roy Acuff. My

friend Norm Engstrom brought the album to me yesterday
on his way home from work. At the moment, Merle Travis
is singing and playing the song "I Am a Pilgrim." He sings,
"I am a pilgrim and a stranger travelin' through this wor-
risome land." I take note, particularly, of his reference to
being a stranger, a stranger and a pilgrim. I will repeat the
song throughout the day. If I could touch the garment, I
believe it would make me whole.

My PHOTOGRAPHY this summer has taken a new and
unexpected turn. I had thought that I would be roaming
the byways of Walworth County finding and photographing the remains — the ruins — of another time. I would
be stopping by the roadside, setting up my tripod, and
taking photographs of barns in various stages of abandon,
rusting farm machinery in fields, falling silos, and vacant
farmhouses. Instead, I am on the pathways I make by foot
around the boundaries of the farm. My photographs are of
landscapes seen from a distance and from very near. I now
see more clearly the place where yet the sweet birds sing.

I seek the essence of the place, at least as seen by my eyes
this special summer. With the care of observation, I see the
sublime in what is close at hand; the extraordinary is found
in the only place it exists, in the ordinary and everyday life.

In my journal, I record a quote I recently read, from
Marcel Proust: "The voyage of discovery is not in seeking

new landscapes but in having new eyes." In the mind's eye, one finds what already exists.

ALL SIGNS point to the cresting of summer. Down at the woods, the red-tailed hawk is teaching its young ones the art of flying and soaring. Another cutting of hay has been taken from the field. In the dryness of mid-summer, the lawn is turning brown, and the daylilies along the road are wilting. Ducks now make their presence known with calls from the pond. Cattails and marsh grasses sway in the afternoon breeze. Elderberries are forming on the clusters that were filled with white flowers only a week or two ago. The groundhogs forage and play in the barnyard all day long. Gravel along the roadside sends up dust when the occasional car passes the farm.

Fireflies light the bean field at night; and last night I heard cicadas singing in the Chinese elms. Finches, wrens, and sparrows preen and bathe—washing the dust from their feathers—in the tray of water I have placed on the walk beside the house. The corn is about to tassel. At supper tonight, I noticed that the days are beginning to get shorter. I found myself singing, already, the first lines of "Autumn Leaves." Summer may be a season, but I am learning to know the seasons within the months of summer.

YES, WHAT HAPPENS happens only once. Nothing
ever occurs again, exactly, the same way or in the same
place. Whether, for me, something occurred in Greenwich
Village, Chapel Hill, Lexington, Providence, or on the farm
in Walworth County, it will never happen again: A walk
one morning with my young daughter across Washington
Square Park; the motorcycle ride through a wooded ravine
in North Carolina; the burial of a family pet high above
the Seekonk River; a meeting with a class of students on a
cold winter day in DeKalb; or driving a load of hay to the
barn on a hot summer afternoon on the farm. Only once,
I am reminded as T. S. Eliot reads from his poem "Ash-
Wednesday" on an audio tape:

> Because I know that time is always time
> And place is always and only place
> And what is actual is actual only for one time
> And only for one place

With Eliot, I rejoice that things are as they are.

THIS WEEK I have been reading about the career of the
photographer Ray K. Metzker, and I have been studying his black-and-white photographs of the natural landscape. I, too, certainly this summer, have sought to frame
the complexity and chaos of the landscape of which I am

an intimate part. Within the confines of the square format I attempt to bring order to the universe. My hope is not to tame nature, but to bring into focus my understanding—or vision—of the world within which I exist. To define my place within the force of nature, as suggested by Metzker in an interview: "Somehow, if there's comprehension of this large force, it humbles those who see it, and even more, those who face it." The sublime is found in the single, ordinary, fleeting moment. In the solitary release of the shutter, the wonder of existence is known.

ALL SUMMER LONG—already I speak of summer as passing—my copy of the *Odyssey* has rested on the corner of the coffee table. I am nearing the end of the book, already well into Book Twenty. And true, as the morning began, "Dawn rose on her golden throne in a sudden gleam of light." Odysseus is gradually making his identity known to his wife Penelope after the long absence. His reentry into the household is as arduous as his many years of travel away from home.

Today in town, heat and humidity will define the day. This morning's *New York Times* tells me that "heat and stifling humidity will persist today from the southern Plains across the Mississippi Valley into the Great Lakes and Ohio Valley." Yet, the paper informs me that in spite of the summer heat, the slide into winter is beginning. We are at the crest of summer this week, and there is nothing I can think of that needs to be done. I am savoring the red raspberries my brother brought to us from his garden.

YESTERDAY I went to the Art Institute in Chicago to see the exhibit of the photographs that Edward Weston made during the last years of his life. I boarded the train in Geneva, after driving from DeKalb, and arrived in Chicago an hour later. I had not been to Chicago for more than a year, since becoming ill last summer. I will think about — and see in my mind's eye — Weston's photographs for some time, I am certain. Today — after yesterday's walk on the streets of Chicago — I am more fatigued than I had expected from an excursion to the city.

Earlier this week, Eudora Welty died, and obituaries and editorials have appeared all week in appreciation of her life. We who work and write with a sense of place, and know the homeplace, find sustenance and encouragement in Eudora Welty. Her stories originate in Jackson, Mississippi, the place that would be her home all her life. Her internal world was soundly grounded: "A sheltered life can be a daring life as well," she wrote, "for all serious daring starts from within."

WE DROVE OVER dark country roads and through the farm towns of central Wisconsin in the humid haze of a summer night. Billie Holiday sang her lonesome, heartfelt songs recorded in the late thirties. A family of deer dashed in front of the headlights. We crossed several times bridges spanning the Rock River. Savoring all the while the Sunday we had spent with my brother and his family — visiting, picnicking on the lawn, and motoring across the lake. A summer night such as this we could wish to last forever.

August

ALL AFTERNOON on the lawn and under the tent we snapped photographs of our family. Some candid and others posed, self-conscious in the taking and the being taken. This morning, after viewing some of the photos, I lay on the sofa reading and looking at the photographs in Wim Wenders's new book *Once.* In the introduction he writes:

> Every photograph is a memento mori,
> Every photograph talks about life and death.

We carried our cameras, as crosses might be worn on chains, around our necks, as reminders of the sacredness of our gathering on a summer's afternoon.

The dog days of summer are evident as August begins. The early Egyptians believed that the appearance of Sirius, the Dog Star, rising with the sun added to the solar heat during the day. Warm and humid southerly winds are to prevail all week. Temperatures are in the mid-90s, and with the humidity factored in, the heat today will seem to be 110 degrees. My labors, fortunately, and as usual, will be indoors.

A YEAR AGO this time I was in a hospital bed hooked up and being treated for a depleted immune system caused by the chronic leukemia that had reached a critical stage in my body. Now a year later, and after treatments and experiments of various kinds, my disease has stabilized, and I am feeling the best I have felt all year.

WE WALKED down the road to the bend, and then along the driveway that led to the house that Kristian and Agnes Skogsbakken had built twenty-five years ago on a pasture and marsh they had bought from Art Johnson. They had emigrated from Norway after they married, and had lived in Illinois until retiring to Wisconsin. Three seasons of the year they lived here, going to Florida for the winter months. Agnes and Kristian were good neighbors and company to my mother all those years. Looking across the field and down the road, she and the Skogsbakkens checked at night for the light in each other's window.

This bright and warm Saturday morning is the day of the auction for the disposal of the Skogsbakkens' worldly goods. A large crowd has already gathered. Cars and trucks are parked for a great distance on both sides of Quinney Road. My cousin Gail is clerking the auction and her husband Dale is high on a ladder on top of the wagon auctioning the first inventory of goods. A lunch wagon has been pulled into the driveway, and the crowd of bidders is attentive to the purpose of the day.

Solveig and I causally browse the contents displayed on the tables lining the hill to the house. The furniture will be the last items to be sold. We talk to neighbors, and I meet someone I had known a half century ago in the Sugar Creek 4-H Club. We talk to the Skogsbakkens' son about the decision to sell the place and its contents. Agnes — in poor health — had moved to Texas to live with her daughter after Kristian died last year.

We do not stay long, although the auction will continue for the rest of the day. Walking back to the farm, rounding the bend in the road, the place rises before us — house, barn, and the tall Chinese elms — like a scene from Brigadoon. A place remote, seemingly in a dream. Maybe it is the heat of the day. One wonders what is real.

At the end of the News Hour, before supper, a woman reads a poem, Robert Frost's "Out, Out—." A boy's hand has been fed into the buzz saw. Under the dark of ether, he gives his last breath, and those who remain listen at his heart:

> Little — less — nothing! — and that ended it.
> No more to build on there. And they, since they
> Were not the one dead, turned to their affairs.

We who remain go about our lives, remembering, but seldom speaking about the lost ones. After a year had passed,

Agnes finally spoke a few words about Kristian. My mother rarely mentioned my father. Occasionally I refer to my mother, gone two years now, and note something about my father, thirty and more years gone. And so it goes, a reluctance to name the dead, perhaps. The pain remains, certainly. The incomprehensibleness of life — and its ending in death — makes us speechless. In the meantime, we turn to the affairs of our daily lives. How else to keep faith in our existence?

I HAVE ALREADY LAID DOWN the tarpaulin to prepare the ground for next year's garden. It will be the first garden we have planted at the farm, except for this year's three tomato plants, which are struggling beside the sheep shed.

I have checked on the health of the peonies planted this spring at the cemeteries. Those protected by the shade trees will definitely survive; the others likely have sufficient root systems to carry them to next spring. Before leaving the Spring Grove Cemetery, standing over the graves of my father and mother, I try to gather some thoughts. The last lines of the poem by Anne Porter, read by Garrison Keillor on the radio this morning, might have sufficed:

> And once we're within her borders
> Death will hunt us in vain.

Still, I grieve, for their sake as well as my own, that my mother and my father are not now alive.

WHEN WE MEET at the Twins Tavern, Jack and Kevin and Heinz and I always ask about each other's health before catching up on the week's events. Other than these weekly get-togethers, I don't go out at night much anymore. If I did, I would like to sing every time the line from Willie Nelson's song: "The night life ain't no good life, but it's my life." I can hear Aretha Franklin singing the line all in blue.

YESTERDAY could just as well have been a dream. Solveig was away in Michigan for the weekend. All day large cumulus clouds moved across the bluest of skies. My friend Dragan soared above, hang gliding over the cornfields of Leland, south of town. In back of the hangar at Harold's Airport, a DC-3 was being outfitted for an around-the-world flight. In the evening, there was a dance in the streets of Sycamore, sponsored by the tavern on the courthouse corner. Well-lit yellow brick buildings enclosed the revelers as in a canyon. The band—rocking and rolling—played from the canopied flatbed truck. Colored lights strobed into the night sky. Paradiso. The band leader shouted out something about Mary. August is the month Midwestern towns celebrate one harvest or another.

WHAT ADVICE WOULD YOU GIVE to someone beyond middle age? I am not thinking about absolutes, about truths that might apply to all aging people under all circumstances. But something that might be a guide to consider under relative conditions. Is not my own keeping of a journal an attempt to tell others — to show others — how one life is being lived with some intention? I hope that I might give inspiration to others in the course of trying to give inspiration to my own life. No absolutes, but encouragements to live our lives before it is too late.

I'm being prompted by today's article in the *New York Times* about the singer and songwriter Mary Chapin Carpenter who has written and recorded songs recently about life at middle age. In one song, she urges her listeners not to "be late for your life." Her lyrics move us beyond the concerns of youth and take us to the threshold of later life. Later life is the stream within which I now swim.

No answer fullblown at one time. Snippets here and there, at best. A few days ago while watching the movie "Beyond Rangoon," I listened carefully to the dialogue between the former Burmese professor and political dissident, portrayed by U Aung Ko, and the young American doctor Laura Bowman, portrayed by Patricia Arquette. At one point, in the garden of a Buddhist monastery, Laura asks the former professor about the right to be happy (she has lost her husband and son). He replies: "We are taught that suffering is the one promise that life always keeps.

So that if happiness comes, we know it is a precious gift which is ours for only a brief time." I know from my years of studying and practicing Buddhism, and from my own life experiences, that life is suffering. Yet each day I look for happiness; I long for moments to be pleasurable. I actually set myself up for suffering with such expectation. In practice, I keep reminding myself that life is simply as it is, without hope of happiness or fear of suffering. To know with awareness that we are alive and that we are living is satisfaction enough. Anything experienced as happiness comes only when unexpected.

IT'S ALL STREAM OF CONSCIOUSNESS, is it not? Even when we get organized to think about something, much of what comes to mind apparently comes from nowhere. As in a night of dreaming, what takes place is out of our control. You wake up in the morning and find that you have been visited in the night by things and people and events that previously were unknown to you. It's the same when you sit down to write; words and sequences of words come to you as never before. Thus the fine line, if any line at all, between remembering and creating anew. From where—great spinner of tales—did last night's dream come? What of this morning's thoughts? We live with the illusion of free will and the pretense of reality. All night long, a gentle summer rain.

NEUTROPHILS AT 2300; stable over the last month—
good. A review of Bobbie Ann Mason's new collection of
stories makes a statement that touches upon my concerns
of late: "Most of these people have reached the plateau of
middle age—a time in life where the past looms as large
as the future and dreams are tempered by regrets." Yes, the
past for me does loom large, and I sense that I have more
past than future. Certainly the distance behind is longer than that ahead. But I am not burdened by regrets.
With enough thought, one can always find regrets, but I
then remember what has given me life rather than what
has taken it away. Flashes of the past come to me regularly—night and day—and give significance to the past. The
past, most of the time, is a source of redemption. The past
is redeemed in remembrance, and the present moment is
thereby redeemed from insignificance. To the farm now, my
bare ruined choir, to plant a pail-full of black-eyed Susans
that I have dug from the backyard—perennials for flower-
ing another year.

WE SIT AT THE KITCHEN TABLE over a late supper listening to a hard rain falling. All afternoon the sky has been
dark, interspersed with sun-laced cumulus clouds. We
watched a large yellow butterfly with wings edged in black
fly back and forth over the timothy field. Crickets were
already jumping in the grass. On the radio, now, we listen

to a program of blues music being broadcast from Memphis on public radio's "American Roots." Jerry Lee Lewis is interviewed ever so briefly, and a recording of his song "Night Train to Memphis" is played. The lyric is repeated, "... singin' hallelujah all the way." Solveig tells me that I am looking the best I have looked all year. Nothing to be blue about tonight. Hallelujah.

NOT A SONGBIRD in sight. Nor a woodchuck or a chipmunk. A moist, warm breeze comes from the east. Butterflies and moths flutter over the hayfield. It is the time of summer when the high-pitched sounds of winged insects fill the air. Grasshoppers abound.

From sunup to sundown, the yellow biplane has been noisily taking off and landing every thirty minutes — busy as a bee, spraying fields this late in the summer. In the evening, the family of Sandhill cranes takes its turn in the sky. A great blue heron flies over the barn on its way to the marsh. My pace this day has been attuned to the late season. A bottle of red wine rests on the kitchen table.

LATE IN THE AFTERNOON we sit in our chairs in Walworth's city park listening to the Jazz Players Big Band. We hear new arrangements of the standards "In the Mood" and "I Can't Get Started." Vacationers, mainly Illinois residents returning from their weekend in Wisconsin, pause for the stoplight at the corner of the park. A yellowing sunlight filters through the branches of the tall oaks.

The morning began, as usual on a Sunday, with the blasts of shotguns coming from the Delavan Sportsman's Club three miles across the marsh. The blasts are interspersed with loud booming noises that come from heavier arms. I compose a letter, finally, and address it to the "opinion" page of the *Delavan Enterprise.* Someday, I assume, with the increase in the number of homes in the area, guns and their noise will not be accepted as they were during the days of the frontier.

Later in the morning, we gathered elderberries that have ripened on the bushes down the road. Solveig spent part of the afternoon preparing the fruit and canning jars of elderberry jam. I planted several elderberry bushes at the edge of the lawn that I have extended north of the house.

We return from the jazz concert in the twilight of the evening. A Sunday in the country, and the sublime has prevailed once again.

I HAVE READ and studied books this month to learn about the art of narration. I have given attention to the first-person narration in Patrick Modiano's autobiographical novel *Dora Bruder,* in Wendell Berry's novel *Jabber Crow,* in Peter Taylor's novel *Summons to Memphis,* and in Jimmy Santiago Baca's memoir *A Place to Stand.* I have also read Herbert McAlexander's new biography of Peter Taylor.

One of the first books that I remember reading, after *The Adventures of Huckleberry Finn,* was the autobiography *Under a Lucky Star* by Roy Chapman Andrews. I must have been a freshman in Delavan High School, and I would have discovered the book in the public library before returning home to the farm in the afternoon after school. I checked last week to see if the library still has the book, to check the date I might have borrowed the book, but the book is no longer on the shelves.

Roy Chapman Andrews was born in nearby Beloit, grew up there, and became a paleontologist who explored the Gobi desert and discovered the eggs of dinosaurs. He was my model of the adventurer, of one who was from Wisconsin but moved beyond to do wonderful things and to become famous. Last week I read the new biography of Andrews by Charles Gallenkamp, *Dragon Hunter.* Years ago when I was young, I discovered Andrews and was inspired, and thought that I too could leave the Midwest and have a life of adventure.

ODYSSEUS still has not made his identity known to his wife. Penelope, as night comes, retires to her bedroom to gain some rest. The goddess Athena, daughter of Zeus and patron of human resourcefulness, gives her comfort. As Homer assures us, "Athena sealed her eyes with welcome sleep." And so we go to bed for welcome sleep at the end of a day of a summer that is fading.

September

A FULL MOON ROSE ABOVE THE RACE TRACK and climbed the far end of the grandstand as night fell and the show began. George Jones, with a fanfare from the Jones Boys, walked onto the stage to the enthusiastic applause and cheers of the crowd. We had secured our seats early, and had waited as the grandstand filled and the time neared for the appearance of the country star. I had purchased his latest album several months ago. Here we were now, with our friends Don and Sally, about to hear the music.

All the years of writing songs, of performing, and of living a life were before us as the lights above the stage flashed from one color to another, ending in blue for the start of another slow number. The aging singer gracefully, and humorously, acknowledged his advancing years, working his life into the long list of songs for which he is known. The lyrical phrases of songs with just the right melodies, sung in a resonant voice that effortlessly moved from high notes to low, came one after another: come take my hand — who's going to fill your shoes — then you oughta be here with me — sweet as strawberry wine — walk through this world with me — living and dying with the choices I've made — he stopped loving her today.

We slowly walked down the steps of the grandstand and left the fairgrounds, made our way to the center of town where we had parked our cars, and parted for home. I remember telling Don that we invest our heroes with qualities that we cannot entirely embody in ourselves. The last days of the fair — coming on Labor Day weekend — always meant that fall was about to begin. And so it seems tonight.

A TRIP — on the back roads — to Lake Geneva has always been a release and a relief from the farm. After a morning of chores, this Labor Day, and a walk up the road to visit an ailing neighbor, we decide to take a little drive to Lake Geneva.

The town by the beautiful lake is a bridge between life on the farm to the northwest and the city life of Chicago to the southeast. For a hundred and some years it has been this way; it was thus when I was growing up; and it is this way today, and likely will be for some time in the future.

After sitting at the bar at Popeye's enjoying a glass of beer, we walk to the city park beside the lake, and standing above the beach we watch the swimmers. In the distance sailboats glide over the sparkling water. To the left is the Riviera with its elegant ballroom where once I danced to Louis Armstrong and his All Stars. I imagine the refrain from "Memories of You." The sweet muted trumpet, the voice, scenes we once knew, and still do.

A FLUSHED FEELING today, aching joints, headache, congestion, a blister, and the side-effects of the Zovirax pills. A swelling under my arm worried me throughout the night. I am assuming and hoping that it is the bite of an insect I found yesterday escaping down my arm.

I have mailed another letter to the editor of the *Delavan Enterprise.*

> We would like to address the problem of the noise that is caused by the gun shots that come from the Delavan Sportsman's Club on County Road P at the crossing at Turtle Creek. We live three miles across the marsh north of the gun club. Especially on weekends, the days are filled with the sound of constant shooting from the gun range. The noise is annoying when we have hopes of pleasant and quiet days. Certainly the shooting has been going on for years. But as we become more conscious of pollution of various kinds, and as the number of residences increases, we are less tolerant of a sport that is becoming a public nuisance. Likely it is time that some community action — perhaps beginning with a survey — is taken. Your suggestions, addressed to this page of the newspaper, would be much appreciated.

We sign and date the letter, and give our address in Sugar Creek Township.

THERE IS SOMETHING ROMANTIC and sublime about the weather forecast for the weekend: "Warm, humid air will spread from the southern Plains to the Midwest on brisk breezes from the southwest. Sunshine will be limited and a few thunderstorms will occur." So much depends upon the weather. I keep reminding myself that we, in our bodies, are ninety percent weather.

I have been looking again at the photographs that Edward Weston made at his home in Carmel and at nearby Point Lobos late in his life. Landscape and family photographs that reflect more than ever the mood of his life. They capture a darkening time, as he is aging and experiencing the first tremors of Parkinson's disease. The Second World War is beginning, his sons are joining the armed forces, and his marriage is beginning to fail. His photographs of the late period show, as David Travis reminds us in the book prepared for the current exhibit at the Art Institute in Chicago, that "here, the quiet lamentation of an accepted fate, rather than the lively celebration of a newly conquered world, seems to determine the resulting character." Travis then quotes lines from the tenth elegy of Rilke's "Duino Elegies." These lines and the ones preceding are as follows:

How we squander our hours of pain.
How we gaze beyond them into the bitter duration
to see if they have an end. Though they are really
our winter-enduring foliage, our dark evergreen,
one season in our inner year—, not only a season
in time—, but are place and settlement, foundation
   and soil and home.

I, too, know the late season, and seek not to squander
it, but to draw from it creatively. A "dark evergreen" season, not only in time, but the foundation and home of my
being. Although, in the dimension of time, the days dwindle down to a precious few — September — I know a season
of the inner year.

FROM UNDER THE PILE of tree trimmings, I pulled out a
portion of the dismantled barnyard fence. We set the newly
created trellis into an existing posthole at the corner of the
plot that is to be our garden. As we poured cement around
the post, a small black salamander scurried out of the hole.
I planted a runner from the trumpet vine back at home in
DeKalb, and Solveig laced it up the post. A remnant of the
past will support orange trumpet blossoms next summer. We
will hang a bird feeder from the beam that extends at a right
angle from the post. Solveig has gone to town for a carton of
milk for the making of pancakes for our breakfast.

A WILD RIDE of a novel: I have just finished reading
Bruce Olds's *Bucking the Tiger,* the telling — the anti-
telling — of the rise and fall of John Henry Holiday, "Doc"
Holiday, known today for his rendezvous at the O. K.
Coral. The Ivy League–trained dentist, quick-on-the-draw
gunman, wanderer, gambler, lover of Kate Elder, generous
tipper, dead of consumption at thirty-five. Olds writes at
the end: "Died in bed, mangled. Died chewed up, chawed
on, dubbed and sore dragooned, both lungs run to whey.
Trounced and trammeled out, all traveled out, at last." Two
passages of poetry quoted in the novel, I report here:

> Man is a museum of diseases, a home of impurities;
> he comes today and is gone tomorrow;
> he begins as dirt
> and departs as stench
>
> — Mark Twain

> he was a handsome man
>   and what i want to know is
> how do you like your blueeyed boy
> Mister Death
>
> — ee cummings

As a young man, John Holiday departed from his home
south of Atlanta on the westbound train. Olds writes: "And
like the aerialist bent to his tightrope, boards his perfect

margin of altitude, reckoning the arc of the slippage in one improvised move a cavalier gesture. This is how history is written: incandescent across the sky in the shift of a single isobar." The story of us all—from beginning, to middle, to end.

YESTERDAY—the 11th of September—will be remembered for a long time, here in this country and around the world. The day that thousands of people perished in the greatest destruction in the United States since the Civil War. This morning's newspaper has a headline that runs in large letters from one side of the page to the other: U.S. ATTACKED: HIJACKED JETS DESTROY TWIN TOWERS AND HIT PENTAGON IN DAY OF TERROR. President Bush, a few minutes ago, called the attack an act of war—with the enemy yet to be determined. The two towers of the World Trade Center have been destroyed, as well as part of the Pentagon, by the hijacked jetliners, and thousands have died a violent death. Throughout the day and night, commentators have repeated that we have entered a new era of national history and that our lives have forever been altered. Today, here at home, one listens to the radio, watches the reporting on television, and wanders about aimlessly in great sorrow. But my problems are inconsequential compared to those of the families and friends of the victims, torn between grieving and the hope of survival.

BEYOND WORDS the images flash across the screen, although many words are attempted by reporters, firemen and police, national leaders, the mayor of New York, the families of victims, and the survivors. Photographers risk their lives and act as witnesses to the violence and destruction, yet stand apart enough to see what they are photographing and to know the significance of what they are doing. The most I can do at the moment, here at home so far from these events, with blood that will not be accepted for donation, is to share a compassionate concern. I will listen to the majesty of Verdi's "Requiem," a music that expresses the range of emotions in time of grief. I will paste a few clippings from today's newspaper into my notebook. I have called my daughters and I have talked to my grandson.

THE SOLACE of a weather report this morning: "An autumnal air mass will sweep from central Canada to the upper Midwest in the wake of a cold front. Chilly breezes will keep temperatures several degrees below normal from the Dakotas to the northern Great Lakes. Widespread frost tonight will end the growing season where winds diminish in much of the upper Midwest." And in the night sky, three bright stars shine in three constellations: Vega in Lyra, Deneb in Cygnus, and Altair in Aquila. In the dark sky, we will be able to look into the edge of the Milky Way galaxy.

Two BANNERS of divergent sentiments were displayed across the street from the National Cathedral in Washington as the services for the National Day of Prayer and Remembrance were taking place. One banner proclaimed — "No war. No retaliation. Stop the violence." The other read — "Today we mourn. Tomorrow we avenge." For the difficult time ahead, I will do all I can in support of the first. Violence will only beget violence.

I must get some rest from the media coverage with the replaying of the images, the continuous analysis, and the President's calls for revenge. Taking to my bed, I am reading a memoir and listening to music on the classical music station, and stopping for long refuges of silence.

I HAVE BEEN DOWN THE ROAD, along the fence line, and to the bottom of the hill to photograph the goldenrod. This time of year, when I was growing up and working in the fields, my father would recite the poem beginning "The goldenrod is yellow." And the goldenrod is yellow again.

OUT OF SORTS all week. I have been keeping close watch on the events — all of the sorrows — that have followed the terrorist attacks. My losses this week are minor compared to the losses of those who lost someone in the tragedy. But I am part of the collective suffering and pain that engulfs the

whole world. I have been unable this week to turn to the
resource in time of need — my journal.

In its own way, the President's address to Congress and
the nation on Thursday night was eloquent. But not long
after its delivery, I had the feeling, a depression actually,
that the country could be on a course of warfare that will
only worsen the problem of terrorism and at the same time
kill innocent people. I, of course, with many of my friends,
oppose terrorism and the values and aims of the terrorists,
but seek a solution that involves international cooperation and justice through a world court. We join together in
opposing both fundamentalist terror and this nation's drive
to war.

TODAY IS THE FIRST FULL DAY of fall for the year
2001. Yesterday the sun crossed the celestial equator, moving from north to south — in other words, the autumnal
equinox has occurred. Sunday the Sabbath offered some
repose and restoration. Early in the morning I practiced
my roping in the backyard, between the house and barn. I
savored the fact that my neutrophils are at 3300, unexpect-
edly high, and that Dr. Williams has encouraged me again
to make hay while the sun shines.

Upon our return to DeKalb, we watched the television
broadcast of the interfaith service for the survivors, held late
in the afternoon at Yankee Stadium. As the service ended,

the flag was raised to full staff, signaling a return to our normal lives. Tonight Antares, the bright star in the constellation Scorpius, will shine in flaming red in the southern sky.

WE WAKE UP to cool mornings and the yellowing light of fall. Today large cumulus clouds have been drifting across a dark blue sky. I thought about the day when I was eight or nine: I was lying in the pasture grass on the hill east of the barn, looking into the formations being created by the white clouds. Suddenly I saw clearly the face of George Washington, and I knew that I had been chosen to do good works in my life. Sixty years later I look into the sky of billowing clouds and simply entertain the mystery of existence.

NOT ONLY DO I KEEP A JOURNAL, but I have chosen to have journals published each time a year of writing has ended. Yet when a book containing my journal entries is published, I have the feeling that I have exposed myself too much to the world. I have made the private public. Writing about my life is motivated by a desire to be a witness to my times. I have the hope that my observations will be of help to others in the living of their lives. And, of course, there is the sheer, primal need to write each day. Maybe in good time I will read my *Borderland* that rests in a box under my desk.

THE COYOTE howls in the night. A loud croaking sound comes from an unknown creature just outside the bedroom window. The furnace now turns on and off throughout the night. In the morning, we awaken to a dense fog that soon dissipates as the sun's rays cut through the moist air. Water drips from the branches of the Chinese elms. The autumn day begins, and we of small harvest welcome a new season on the farm.

We spend the afternoon cleaning out the milk house that is attached to the barn. Several years of accumulated tools and milking utensils, obsolete and rusting, are pulled into the barn and deposited on the musty straw in the stalls once occupied by the cows, horses, bull, and heifers. Next spring the cleaned-out milk house will serve as our gardening shed.

Late in the afternoon bluebirds fly to the new bird bath north of the house. The birds bathe furiously, flapping their wings, preening, and puffing their breasts to the fading sun. A lone phoebe moves among the branches of the lilac bush. Ten robins gather on the gravel driveway. I take a few photographs of the drying corn in the field to the west.

In the evening we watch a rerun of Guy Lombardo and the Royal Canadians playing the songs of the forties and fifties, "Too Marvelous for Words," "Far Away Places," and "Someone to Watch Over Me." September ends as the days and nights dwindle down.

October

THE LEGENDARY HARVEST MOON rose as scheduled shortly after sunset this evening. The full moon will traverse the sky during the night, and there are promises that it will be visible in the western sky when we wake up in the morning. Called the Harvest Moon because it is the closest full moon to the autumnal equinox, and because the moon once furnished light for farmers before tractors with headlights arrived. With the Harvest Moon shining, farmers could reap their harvest all night long. But as the new month begins this year, since the events of September 11th, we are living in a sort of limbo, not knowing what may happen next. For the time being, we are beyond the comforts of celestial certainties.

ALL YEAR I have been waiting to record in my journal a few lines from the poem by John Keats titled "To Autumn." In the fall of 1819, Keats sent a letter to a friend, and with the letter he enclosed the poem. In the letter he wrote: "How beautiful the season is now — How fine the air. I never liked stubble-fields so much as now — Aye better than the chilly green of the spring. Somehow, a stubble-field looks warm—in the same way that some pictures look warm." Lines from the first stanza of the poem:

> Season of mists and mellow fruitfulness,
>   Close bosom-friend of the maturing sun;
> Conspiring with him how to load and bless
>   With fruit the vines that round the thatch-eves run.

The poem ends: "The red-breast whistles from a garden-croft; / And gathering swallows twitter in the skies." Who does not enjoy the twitter of gathering swallows in the skies?

SINCE FRIDAY MORNING we have been on the road. All day we drove through Wisconsin to reach St. Paul by night-fall. Our purpose was to attend the annual trade show of the Upper Midwest Booksellers Association being held in the River Center. The University of Wisconsin Press had asked me to be at their booth to sign copies of my *Borderland* book. During the hour of signing, I disposed of the sixty copies that had been brought to the trade show. In the evening, we danced in the streets of St. Paul and watched as Garrison Keillor hosted a program outside the Fitzgerald Theater. There was a loon-calling contest as well as cajun and country music in the cool of the night.

Traveling along the banks of the Mississippi River on Sunday morning, we heard the first reports of the shelling and bombing of Taliban sites in Afghanistan, the obvious beginning of the war on terrorism. We stopped for relief at the Wollersheim Winery near Prairie du Sac, where the annual wine-stomping festival was taking place. Samples of the year's harvest were being offered, and we purchased bottles of Dumaine du Sac, a dry red wine from grapes grown on the hillsides that rise above the winery. Hundreds of connoisseurs walked gleefully out of the vineyards as the sun was setting over the Wisconsin River Valley. We were back at the farm later in the evening, listening to the wind-blown rattle of dry corn leaves outside the bedroom window.

YESTERDAY Solveig and I spent the day with our realtor in Madison looking for a house to buy. We have entertained the possibility of living in Madison for some time. Today I am checking on the financial details of a move, a move that will place us closer to the farm and, at the same time, in a larger city, the state's capitol.

In the meantime, thirty Sandhill cranes circle high above the farm, gathering in a flock for the fall migration to the south. Later, thirteen wild turkeys crossed the road as we rounded the bend; and they walked into the woods at the edge of the marsh.

Air strikes continue over the Afghan city of Kabul, and

against other sites assumed to be of military importance. While working in the garage yesterday, preparing tools for the coming winter, we heard a loud sonic boom that shook the house. I read in this morning's newspaper that a Boeing 767 carrying 153 passengers, on a flight from Los Angeles to Chicago's O'Hare airport, was met by fast-flying fighter jets, dispatched to deal with a passenger trying to force his way into the cockpit of the passenger jet. One remembers the President's order to shoot down any passenger plane that is being hijacked. Fortunately for everyone, the deranged passenger was subdued before reaching the cockpit. We had run out of the garage and looked into the sky to see what was the matter.

CRIMES AGAINST HUMANITY—as were the attacks of September 11th—should be the jurisdiction of an international tribunal and court, not the unilateral revenge by a single nation. I have ordered a United Nations flag if a flag is to be flown.

The remedy for terrorism is, of course, one that is long-term. I like the full-page announcement in yesterday's *New York Times,* sponsored by the Art of Living Foundation, an educational and humanitarian organization recognized by the United Nations and active in 132 countries around the world.

Today, terrorism is a global social concern. As a long-term remedy, we need to educate the entire population of the world to:

— Value life itself more than religion, race or culture.
— Live the human values of friendliness, compassion, cooperation and a sense of belonging to all people.
— Honor diversity and appreciate all religious and cultural traditions, for the world will not be safe if even a small pocket of people is left ignorant or fanatical.
— Adopt practical methods to release stress and tension in life; stress is the root cause of all conflict and violence.
— Have confidence that we can achieve change through peaceful and non-violent means.

With the postscript, "Know God is with us all."

THE NOBEL PEACE PRIZE has been awarded to the United Nations and to its Secretary General, Kofi Annan. In the announcement of the peace prize, the Nobel committee noted that the body "wishes in its centenary year to proclaim that the only negotiable route to global peace and cooperation goes by way of the United Nations." In the wake of the attacks, and the on-going military response being waged by the United States, the recognition of the international organization is significant. I await the morning mail for the arrival of the United Nations flag that I have ordered. I have heard recently a quote from Socrates: "I am not a citizen of Athens or Greece, I am a citizen of the world."

The Nobel Prize in Literature has been awarded to V. S. Naipaul. We are reminded that in books of fiction and nonfiction Naipaul has explored the themes of exile, dislocation, the dilemmas of post-colonial societies, and the confusions of the present. Reading his autobiographical novel *The Enigma of Arrival* was important to my own development and to my sense of self and of the times. The newspaper quotes from his book *A Way in the World,* a work that mixes novel and memoir, history and imagination: "Most of us know the parents or grandparents we come from. But we go back and back, forever; we go back all of us to the very beginning; in our blood and bone and brain we carry the memories of thousands of beings … We cannot understand all the traits we have inherited. Sometimes we can be strangers to ourselves."

I will order today Naipaul's new novel *Half a Life.* The newspaper ends its article on the announcement of the literature prize: "V. S. Naipaul is a literary circumnavigator, only ever really at home in himself, in his inimitable voice."

OUR OFFER TO PURCHASE a house in Madison has been accepted. After years of carefully considering a move, the decision has been made. We will be starting a new life as this year ends and a new one begins. In the meantime, let us keep focused on the tasks at hand, and keep the anxiety of change in check. We will continue to maintain our valued friendships in DeKalb, visiting this place often where Solveig has lived for fifty years and I for eighteen. Since leaving the farm for college, this is the place I have lived for the longest period of time. This town on the prairie in northern Illinois has been a nurturing source for a significant portion of our lives.

IN THE WEEKS since the terrorist attacks, people have turned to poetry for consolation. One mourner in New York posted lines from W. B. Yeats:

> All the words that I utter,
> And all the words that I write,
> Must spread out their wings untiring,
> And never rest in their flight,
> Till they come where your sad, sad heart is.

This is a poetic lament that extends to all who are witnesses to the times.

I AM ON MY WAY to visit Anne in Oxford, Mississippi.
Solveig drove me to O'Hare in the morning, and Anne
will meet me at the airport in Memphis. We will drive
to Oxford where she is teaching at the University of
Mississippi.

Before boarding the United flight at O'Hare, I ordered
a cup of soup and a glass of beer at a restaurant on the con-
course. The waitress at the bar, to my great surprise, asked
to see my I.D. I haven't been asked to identify my age for
a long time. The waitress looked at my driver's license and
laughed.

On the way to O'Hare, I had called the hematology
nurse at the University of Wisconsin Hospital to find out
the results of my lab test of the day before, and had learned
that my white count and my neutrophils were still at a good
level.

VISIONS OF MISSISSIPPI linger as gale winds blow
cold air over the Great Lakes. Rain yesterday and today,
and snow flurries are in the forecast for this afternoon and
evening. All of this with new infections of Anthrax being
reported daily.

The trip to Oxford has inspired me to read more of
William Faulkner. I walked through his house and over
the grounds of Rowan Oak, where he lived from 1930 to
the time of his death in 1962. His study at the back of the

house remains as he left it: a small table near the window with pencils and typewriter, the table given to him by his mother; his Adirondack chair and bed; books on the shelf, including a volume of T. S. Eliot's poetry; and written on the wall, Faulkner's outline for *A Fable,* the novel that takes place during Holy Week.

I closely observed the stable that Faulkner had built with his own hands to house his horses and to store hay for them. At the foot of his bed on the second floor of the house were his riding boots, and on the mantel were his two cameras.

The next evening Anne and I went to St. Peter's Cemetery and found the graves of Faulkner and his wife Estelle. A partly consumed bottle of Jack Daniel's whiskey rested on the gravestone. I spent the next morning at Square Books reading passages from Faulkner's novels. Beyond the novelist, I was happy to find Anne nicely settled at the university. We drove to Memphis in the morning for the flight home.

I HEARD ON THE RADIO that the Jesuit-educated poet John L'Heureus said the following about being a writer: "The whole idea of being a writer is to get out of oneself into another hide." My own writing, it seems, is not to get out of this self but to raise it to a different level. I become something more than my regular self when I write. William

Faulkner once remarked about the writer, "He is one thing when he is a writer and he is something else while he is a denizen of the world." The inner self comes forth in the process of writing.

When I think of myself before the age of thirty, and often when I am at the farm, I am very much an "Earl." When I think of myself as a mature adult, I am "Richard." Yet I would not be myself today, my whole self, if I did not have these two selves. It is interesting to me that I have insisted on maintaining these two identities. A great relief it is to me when I sit down at my desk to write, where union is made.

BEFORE DAWN the planets Mercury and Venus, within a degree of each other from our perspective here on Earth, accompany one another in the eastern sky. We make our way to Chicago to attend the matinee performance of Kurt Weill's "Street Scene" at the Lyric Opera. First performed in 1946, with a libretto by Langston Hughes, the opera is regarded by some as America's first real opera. In the elevator, on our way up to the seats in the second balcony, the operator tells us that we are going to the "sky boxes."

The full moon rises just behind us as we drive home. We will arise tomorrow morning to a new month, and to the day known as All Saints Day. A day traditionally celebrated as a reminder of the hope for entry into heaven.

November

THIS IS THE MONTH for the slantwise telling of tales. "Tell all the truth," Emily Dickenson wrote, "but tell it slant." She concludes her poem: "The Truth must dazzle gradually / or every man be blind." The truth of the matter can surprise even the teller.

What I am trying to say is that we—in this little household—are on the move. Before the month is over the contents of our house in DeKalb must be packed and ready to transport north to the farm and to Madison. As the month ends, if all goes as planned, we will be living in a different house, the house we have purchased in Madison. Our leave will have been taken of DeKalb; our familiar home will be abandoned. And we will begin the long process of making another house a home. The truth of the move will be experienced—and told—with the remove of slant. How else to survive the rending asunder, even for desired ends?

PACKING. Boxes marked variously — RQ Books, SQ Books, Kitchen Utensils, Dishes, Knickknacks, Storage. Other boxes contain paintings, framed photographs, and tools from the workshop. We will carry large breakable items—mirrors, lamps, pottery—in the back seat of the car. A professional mover will take the furniture in a van.

The mind is scattered, as are the belongings of a lifetime. I must remind myself to stay focused. Last night I told Solveig to remember that we are experiencing a significant moment in our lives. House closings—here and there—are set for the last week of the month.

IN A DISCUSSION on the radio of the portrayal of war in books, one commentator quoted Walt Whitman to the effect that the real world never gets into the books. Books, by their very essence, are removed from the primary events and actions. But they are themselves events and actions, written by real-life authors. Mention books, now that I am making decisions about which ones to pack and which ones to dispose of, and you have my complete attention.

Most hardcover books I will save and pack into boxes for the move north. Paperbacks that age faster than hardcover books, even paperback editions of my own books, I tend to place in the discard pile that is fast growing on the basement floor. Academic books are more likely to go into the pile than literary books. I save most biographies, autobiographies, and memoirs. Nature books have a good chance of surviving the cut. And there are the books of sentimental value that will be saved, books given to me as gifts by friends and family. And there are those books that have been crucial to me at various points in my life; they will be boxed and transported for later shelving. The books that I discard will go to public libraries for their collections or annual fund-raising sales. Each book has played a part in the living of my life. Books discarded are given my blessing as they enter the cardboard box.

WHAT A DIFFERENCE a week makes in the passing of November. Last week the corn was being picked at the farm. This week the fields are entirely in stubble. An antlered deer stands tall on the hill at the far end of the harvested soybean field.

With the aid of a rented U-Haul truck, we have moved a load of goods from our soon-to-be-vacated house in DeKalb. At the farm, we have walked to the woods to post No Hunting signs, the bow-and-arrow season for deer being in full swing. Solveig has called the County Sheriff to report hunters sitting in trees waiting for deer to pass below.

The roving reporter for Delavan's weekly newspaper has asked the question, "How have you changed since September 11?" One older man gave the following answer:

> Can I tell you about something that recently happened to me? I lost my wife on Sept. 24. We were married 47 years. I look at the world's problems and

> that's one thing. And then there are the personal
> things. But if you want to know what changed my
> life, losing my wife changed my life. I feel lost.

Solveig volunteered her response to the question, saying
that she had become more accepting of what once could be
a source of irritation. I said that since September 11th I have
not been interested in watching movies — on TV, video, or
at a theater. Real life is life enough.

ANNE'S BIRTHDAY TODAY — born in 1970 in New York
City. As I sit here at my desk, she is speaking to the faculty
at Duke University about her recent translation of a work by
the French psychoanalyst, J.B. Pontalis. In Paris, Pontalis had
suggested to Anne that she might be seeking a father substitute in her translation. Likely I have this a bit inexact, but
the mysteries of translation — and transference — remain. As
well as the mysteries of being a father.

WE HAD SET THE ALARM CLOCK for 4:00 AM. When
it rang, we slipped on our clothes and made our way to the
far side of the barn where there was darkness away from the
yardlight. The Leonid meteor shower was under way. The
meteors, which were actually pieces of the comet Tempel-
Tuttle, flashed across the sky. More than the occasional

shooting star we sometimes see in the night sky, we saw at least two streaks of light each minute. We leaned against the silo as a fresh breeze came out of the south. Condensation from the night's dew dropped from the high eaves of the barn. After a half-hour of gazing and delighting, we returned to the kitchen for a cup of coffee, and then went to bed for another four hours of sleep. It was the soundest sleep of the night.

I CONTINUE my night reading of V. S. Naipaul's new novel *Half a Life*. The half a life is the life of a great part of the world's population. Whether you are a refugee, a migrant to another land, or someone who has moved from one class or culture to another, or you have moved from one town to another, you are experiencing half a life — for at least part of the time. A good portion of your life is borrowed or defined for you by others. Naipaul, in an interview, has said that he escaped some of his half-life by being a writer. A writer invents a life in the process of imagination and the construction of a narrative that is committed to paper, whether in a journal or in a published book. In the writing of both fiction and nonfiction, one is constructing a life.

Asked what themes he will evoke in his acceptance speech for the Nobel award, Naipaul said: "My background is at once exceedingly simple and exceedingly complicated.

The complication comes in the writing and exploration of that simple background." Writing moves the writer from simple existence to a reflection on, and exploration of, that existence. The reality of life is both mined and imagined, and recreated to make a life whole.

THE REPORT is that three-fourths of Afghanistan is now controlled by the Northern Alliance and the military forces of the United States. The southern city of Kandahar is under siege, and the Taliban are fleeing. The search for Osama bin Laden has taken to the mountains and into the caves.

Here at home I am packing what seems to be a lifetime of possessions. Yesterday I took ten boxes of books to the university library — a donation to the annual sale of books. I hastily retrieved my aging undergraduate textbook on the anatomy and physiology of the human body, telling the librarian that the book reminds me of what I learned about sex in college.

There are many other worldly possessions that I must discard, relegating them to the dustbin of history. I cautiously place some of the handwritten manuscripts for several of my books into the recycle box. The State Historical Society of Wisconsin has already committed the manuscripts to microfilm. Other things are thrown away, never to be seen again. With each disposal, I practice my own mortality. Goodbye to all of that.

THE END OF NOVEMBER WEATHER this 2001 year:
cool, windy, scattered showers, and the possibility of snow
flurries. And this year, in addition to the weather forecasts,
there is the move that we are making which will change our
lives in unknown and unpredictable ways. There is nothing like a move to make one realize how precious life is,
and how precarious. When my body and mind and spirit
ached from exhaustion and anxiety, I went to Urgent Care
and asked the attending physician for a prescription of
Lorazepam. Finally a good sleep last night.

We travel with cartons of breakable treasures between
what was once home in DeKalb, to the ever-present farm,
and on to the new house in Madison. At the house-clos-
ing ceremonies in Madison on Monday, Solveig and I both
remarked that we felt like resident aliens from another
world.

STAY CLOSE to the moment; stray not far from the details
of this day. To give us some continuity with the past, however — and grounding in spiritual wisdom — we watched
a rerun on public television of Bill Moyer's interviews with
Joseph Campbell on the power of myth. We are reminded
that the eternal is in the present moment — rather than
someplace far away in an everlasting life after death. How
often have I experienced, really experienced, the eternal in the present moment? Fortunately, quite often. But

once would be enough to know the eternal. Eternity burns brightly in an instant of everyday life.

December

THE WEATHER FORECASTERS are saying that the last thirty days have been the warmest in the history of record-keeping in this part of the country. December begins in a mist, and there is the promise of sunshine later in the day. A redheaded woodpecker searches for insects on the bark of the Chinese elm. We move back and forth between three places, in a camping mode, from a near-empty house in DeKalb, to the farmhouse packed with boxes, to the house in Madison that is slowly shaping up as home.

The main roads into Kandahar are being cut off by troops supported by American air power. The front page of the morning newspaper carries a color photograph of refugees gathered around small tents set in the sand. I will clip the photograph from the paper, fold it and place it in my billfold to remind me of those who travel under circumstances much less fortunate than ours.

THREE CAMELS WITH RIDERS dressed as the Magi strolled down the streets of Elkhorn in the annual Christmas parade. Floats, ponies hitched to carts, and members of a marching band seated on a flatbed truck filled the streets for over an hour on a snowless, windy, sunny day. At home on the farm, in the early evening, Solveig and I for the first time

during the week—with our material household in
disarray—talked again about the wisdom of our move.

A TUB OF FRESHLY PULLED RADISHES was placed
on a chair inside the front door of Tubby's Too tavern on
Country Trunk A. We had stopped earlier in the evening
for a glass of beer on our way back to the farm. The hopeful
grower sat at the bar watching from the corner of his eye for
possible buyers of his radishes. We took comfort being in
the company of fellow travelers and revelers.

IF I WERE TO WRITE A LETTER to each of my friends
in DeKalb, as I am feeling the need to do right now, I
would say something like the following: First, I want to
express my thankfulness for years of friendship, friendships that I very much want to continue. Second, the move
has been more difficult—both physically and emotional-
ly—than I had anticipated. Third, the move away from
familiar surroundings reorients one; my taken-for-granted
assumptions have become clearer, and my awareness of
everyday things has heightened. Fourth, I feel the need for
renewed attention to my spiritual being; where this will lead
I cannot at the moment imagine, but the need is keenly felt
once again. And fifth, I remember and cherish the visits
of my friends to the house to see and comfort me during

the critical time of my illness. I will be ready to give care to others when care is needed. I hope to be a good friend.

IN AN INTERVIEW in the *New York Times*, the neurologist and writer Oliver Sacks says that the love of order is a great delight, and that writing is an important bulwark against chaos. He adds that he has to write to come to terms with experience in one way or another. Writing for me, also, is the search for order, the keeping of chaos at bay, and the processing of my own experiences. And in the telling, I hope in some small way to help others.

I PURCHASED THE COIN PURSE at the leather store, filled it with quarters, and made my way to the bus stop for Bus NO. 7. It was my first venture as a resident of Madison to the Capitol Square, although for more than half a century I had gone to the Square on one occasion or another.

I remember with great fondness the grade-school trip we made in 1946 to visit the Capitol building and to the state office to shake hands with Governor Goodland. I rode in the car driven by my mother. It was snowing that day, and we watched intensely from the car window as we passed farmhouses, roadside taverns, and wooded fields. We drove home on a dark night as snow fell heavily from the sky.

As a graduate student in the late 1950s, I walked

uptown—along State Street—passing used bookstores, men's clothing stores, art supply stores, and movie theaters. Once in winter, I walked in a snowstorm to hear Bob Scobie and his Dixieland band play into the night. In recent years, Solveig and I have driven to Madison to gather provisions at the farmer's market held on Saturdays around the Square.

Yesterday, before catching the NO. 7 bus for my return home, I had lunch at a Himalayan restaurant. I then purchased a small Buddha statue as a gift for my daughter and strolled to the end of State Street. Along the way I noticed that the bookstores were featuring my book in the window. I enjoyed a cup of coffee at a café before the bus pulled up at the waiting station. I was let off a half block from my house, a senior citizen returning from an outing.

I'M ALL SHOOK UP. There are times in one's life—and this is such a time in mine—when life is out of joint, when one is at loose ends, and daily life lacks a basic rhythm. Certainly I was seeking a reordering of my life. But I had forgotten the pain that naturally accompanies change that comes with the disturbance in familiar surroundings and routines. I remind myself—in the middle of the storm—that everything has a price.

At night, at the farm, I find solace in a walk to the barn. The Buddha figure that I have recovered from one of the packed boxes in the farmhouse will help bring me to the attention and awareness I now need. May there be compassion toward all others near and far, as well as toward myself. Practice loving kindness.

I MADE CERTAIN to visit friends on a return trip to DeKalb. We attended a party celebrating the birth of Solveig's little granddaughter. Beforehand, Al and Cele Meyer walked over to the empty house — our house that still has not been sold — and we sat in front of the fireplace in our camping chairs. Later in the evening I met Jack at the Twins, where we talked about the move to Madison. Earlier on the phone, Jack had jokingly referred to me as a traitor for leaving, a comment I had been taking seriously. He assured me it was his own interest that was being expressed, his own desire to have me in town. I am feeling sorry we will not be seeing each other as often and as easily as before.

We observed that we are both contructionists, that any meaning in this world is created by us as human beings. There are no absolutes outside the human mind. We both wish for an ultimate meaning, but I am the one that has had a lifetime of searching for something that transcends this mortal life. My move is another attempt to find new — or renewed — interest in the meaning of my life. I seek to know new things, to make discoveries that did not seem to be forthcoming in the old place. I am working on faith alone; Sisyphus is rolling the stone up the hill.

A SENSE THIS MORNING that a cloud may be lifting from the travails of moving. I awoke this morning at the farm with an inner peace that has been escaping me these last few days. The sun steams through the lace curtains in the south window of the farmhouse, making patterns on the living room walls. A prism high in one of the windows sends rainbow colors dancing on the ceiling. I will take a morning walk along the fence line, and make my way to the stone pile in the far corner of the field to fetch a rock that I can take back with me to Madison. We will load the car again and head north along the back roads, accepting the blessings that come gracefully.

SAINT LUCIA DAY TODAY. Patron saint of sight, and namesake of the feast day that starts the Christmas season in Scandinavia. Last night Solveig and I sat before the lighted fireplace on camp chairs in our DeKalb house and toasted the continuing saga of our adventure in the changing of place and home.

Kofi Annan has accepted the Nobel Peace Prize and has delivered his address, noting: "In the 21st Century, I believe the mission of the United Nations will be defined by a new, more profound awareness of the sanctity and dignity of every human life, regardless of race or religion." He observed that the old problems that existed on September 10th, before the attacks, are still with us, namely the elimination of poverty, the fight against H.I.V. and AIDS, and the question of the environment. And peace must be made real and tangible in the daily life of every individual. "Peace must be sought, above all, because it is the condition for every member of the human family to live a life of dignity and security."

How to live a meaningful and truthful life, is that not the essence of our being human? We hope, as we grow older, that we will not live and die meaninglessly. I am reminded of this again and again in my reading of *Buddhadhamma,* the book translated by Grant Olson. He gave me a copy of the book—having inscribed it "with metta"—as I took my leave from DeKalb. The way ultimately may be pathless, but there are directions offered in the wisdom of the Buddha.

I met a man—yesterday, while sitting in the atrium of the Hilldale Mall in Madison. He sat down beside me to rest his sore knees. We talked about ailments we had in common, and about where we live, our work histories, and our grown children. Time passed quickly, and we eventually parted without ever introducing ourselves to each other. All I know is that he had come to Madison from Janesville on a shopping trip with his wife—and that likely we will never meet again. One thing I know for certain is that the next time I meet and share time with a stranger, I will take care to exchange names and express the possibility that we might meet again.

THIS MORNING, droplets of water hang on the branches of the locust tree just beyond the balcony of our new house. In a leisurely manner, we prepare to attend the Sunday morning services at the First Unitarian Society of Madison. For a long time—since my days as a graduate student in the 1950s—I have admired and visited the building designed by Frank Lloyd Wright.

The theme for this morning's service is solitude. May Sarton is quoted:

> Solitude is not all exaltation and inner space
> Where the soul breathes and work can be done.
> Solitude exposes the nerve, raises up ghosts.
> The past, never at rest, flows through it.

And the reading is for Hanukah, during the lighting of the Menorah: "Grateful for small miracles, we rejoice in the wonder of light and darkness." The sermon is an exploration of loneliness and solitude, and how the two are part of the spiritual journey. The day is cloudy and a rain is softly falling, a good day for both solitude and communion with others.

It is ironic that one who is noted as having such a firm sense of place is intentionally disrupting that sense of place by changing places. I read an advertisement for my book in the *Ruminator Review:* "Equal parts memoir, geography, photo journal, and natural history, *Borderland* is a nuanced literary evocation of place, a deeply felt exploration of what it means to be at home in a particular landscape." I am still in the familiar landscape of the Midwest, but what a difference a few miles can make in one's sense of place. Someday, I assume, I will be at home in this place to which I have moved. But perhaps my most familiar landscape is the borderland itself.

The bust i have unpacked of James Joyce now has a prominent place on the top shelf of the bookcase in my study. Garrison Keillor on "The Writer's Almanac" has quoted Edna O'Brien on her first reading of Joyce's *A Portrait of the Artist as a Young Man.* She said: "Reading it was the most astonishing literary experience of my life. What I learned was that as a writer one must take material from life, from the simple, indisputable, and often painful world about one, and give it somehow its transfiguration, but at the same time shave all excess and untruth form it, like peeling a willow." Yes, to take the material from everyday life and transfigure it into the written word. Such is my labor as I sit at my writing desk with James Joyce looking down from the high shelf.

AN OWL HOOTED from the elm as I woke up in the middle of the night at the farm. A night of little sleep, thinking about my doctor's recommendation that I take another round of Rituxan after the holidays. My blood counts are good, but the doctor wants to avoid having to "dodge the bullet" of a year ago when my life was threatened. This is a reminder that I really am chronically ill.

This is the first day of winter — the day of the winter solstice. On this day, the northern hemisphere is farthest from the sun. Garrison Keillor reminds me on his program this morning that today is the birthday of Edward Hoagland, the author of one of my favorite books, *The Courage of Turtles*. Hoagland has said the following about the necessity of writing: "I love life and believe in its goodness and rightness, but I seem not to be terribly well fitted for it — that is, not without writing. Writing is my rod and staff. It saves me, exults me." I too am thus saved.

I ASSUME THAT THE WRITING — my writing — will continue as long as I exist. But I also know that I am entering
a stage of my life where contact with others — beyond the
writing — is increasingly important. I wake in the night
wishing to see my daughters, my brother, other family
members, and old friends. This sense of dependence, or
interdependence, on others is the strongest I have known
for years. A grace recently bestowed.

A SNOW CAME IN THE NIGHT, the latest first snowfall
of the season on record. To the farm we must go, I said, to
take the winter photographs that are needed for my book.
Once at the farm, with the camera mounted on the tripod,
and flakes of snow blowing across the lens, I focused on
marsh and hills. With the temperature well below freezing,
the shutter dropped slowly. Chickadees, nuthatches, and a
red-bellied woodpecker were eating from the suet blocks as
I returned to the house.

   As we left the farmhouse for our return to Madison, I
paused in the living room to remember — and give thanks
for — the dear family that gathered here on Christmas Eves
past — after chores had been completed for the night.

IT CAME UPON A MIDNIGHT CLEAR — glorious songs of
old, and the hope for peace on earth. Christmas this year

takes place in the midst of the war that is being waged in Afghanistan and in the Mideast. Reconstructed images come to mind when we hear the stories of refugees in the desert. A Buddhist abbot, Thanissaro Bhikkhu, writing in the current issue of *Tricycle,* gives wise counsel: "When the winds of change reach hurricane force, our inner refuge of mindfulness, concentration, and discernment is the only thing that will keep us from being blown away." He continues: "When the basis of our well-being is firm within, we act with true courage and compassion for others, for we're coming from a solid position of calmness and strength." At the end of last week we of the Interfaith Network in DeKalb stood on the corner of Lincoln Highway and First Street as witnesses for a peaceful solution to the crises around the world.

We celebrate Christmas at home in Madison this year with visits from Solveig's daughters and their families. I have talked on the telephone with Laura and Anne, Billy, Daniel, and little Julian — calls to and from Boston and Oxford, Mississippi. A cold night, snow on the ground, and a warm bed. I make a prayer for the night from the words of Thanissaro Bhikku:

> So take heart. Do what you can to help the living,
> and dedicate the merit of your practice to the dead.
> We may be powerless to change the past, but we do
> have the power to shape the present and the future

by what we do, moment to moment, right now. And in maintaining our intention to be as skillful as possible in thought, word, and deed, we'll find the only true refuge there is.

THE MOON IS FULL and the temperature is below zero. Shadows of tree trunks and branches fall on the snow between house and barn. A buck deer stands in the moonlight. I tap on the window and the deer runs across the field and into the woods.

A year has passed. I have kept watch. In the scheme of things, the year is a blink of the eye of the universe. I have thought all year, while keeping watch, about Isaac Watts's rendering of Psalm 90:4:

> A thousand ages in thy sight
> Are like an evening gone;
> Short as the watch that ends the night
> Before the rising sun.

Night watch—and thoughts late in the night. Most wondrous for all of that.

LET US NOT FORGET the journey of Odysseus at year's end. The last part of the *Odyssey* is a drama of identity disguised and identity revealed. Back on the island of Ithaca, Odysseus is gradually recognized by his son, his old dog Argos, who is now too old to approach him but wags his tail in recognition, and his nurse Eurycleia who recognizes him by a scar on his body. His wife Penelope finally welcomes her husband to the bed, and Odysseus, with wife in his arms, knows joy: "Joy, as warm as the joy that shipwrecked sailors feel when they catch sight of land." In the morning, Dawn with her rose-red fingers shines upon their happiness.

As prophesied earlier in his journey, the final end will ultimately come for Odysseus. He will travel inland, carrying an oar on his shoulder, until he reaches a place where people are ignorant of the sea and ships. Odysseus will plant his oar in the ground and make his sacrifices to the gods. And at last:

> And at last my own death will steal upon me …
> a gentle, painless death, far from sea it comes
> to take me down, borne down with the years in
>   ripe old age
> with all my people here in blessed peace around me.
> All this, the prophet said, will come to pass.

NEW YEAR'S EVE. The odyssey of the year 2001 is about to end. Fortunately, there will be a journey into another year. For the time being, early in the morning as the low sun casts its ray between the house and the barn, with the temperature at five above zero, I quickly bundle up in my jacket and go out to take a few more photographs.

During the passing of the year, as storyteller, I have been like the Knight in Geoffrey Chaucer's *Canterbury Tales*. Whether by chance or fate or accident, I have drawn the shortest cut, and I have told the tale that I had sworn to tell. What more is there to say? Until some other time.

Bibliography

Amis, Martin. *Experience.* London: Jonathan Cape, 2000.

Baca, Jimmy Santiago. *A Place to Stand.* New York: Grove Press, 2001.

Bernstein, Richard. *Ultimate Journey.* New York: Alfred A. Knopf, 2001.

Berry, Wendell. *Jabber Crow.* Washington: Counterpoint, 2000.

Berry, Wendell. *A Timbered Choir: The Sabbath Poems 1979 – 1997.* Washington: Counterpoint, 1998.

Bhagavad Gita. Trans. Stephen Mitchell. New York: Harmony Books, 2000.

Bly, Robert. "The Cabbages of Chekhov," *The Night Abraham Called to the Stars.* New York: HarperCollins, 2001.

Browne, Janet. *Charles Darwin: A Voyage, Vol. I.* New York: Alfred A. Knopf, 1995.

Camus, Albert. *The First Man.* Trans. David Hapgood. New York: Alfred A. Knopf, 1995.

Cather, Willa. *The Professor's House.* New York: Vintage Books, 1990 (1925).

Chaucer, Geoffrey. *The Canterbury Tales.* Trans. Nevill Coghill. Baltimore: Penguin Books, 1962.

Chekhov, Anton. *Five Plays.* Trans. Ronald Hingley. New York: Oxford University Press, 1980.

Coleridge, Samuel Taylor. *The Rime of the Ancient Mariner.* Ed. Paul H. Fry. Boston: Bedford/St.Martin's, 1999.

Darwin, Charles. *Voyage of the Beagle: Charles Darwin's Journal of Researches.* Eds. Janet Browne and Michael Neve. New York: Penguin Books, 1998.

Eliot, T. S. *The Complete Poems and Plays of T. S. Eliot.* London: Faber and Faber, 1969.

Frank, Arthur W. *The Wounded Storyteller: Body, Illness, and Ethics.* Chicago: University of Chicago Press, 1995.

Frost, Robert. *Collected Poems, Prose, and Plays.* New York: Library of America, 1995.

Gallenkamp, Charles. *Dragon Hunter: Roy Chapman Andrews and the Central Asiatic Expeditions.* New York: Viking, 2001.

Gao Xingjian. *Soul Mountain.* Trans. Mabel Lee. New York: HarperCollins, 2000.

Gillick, Muriel R. *Lifelines: Living Longer, Growing Frail, Taking Heart.* New York: W. W. Norton, 2001.

Hoagland, Edward. *The Courage of Turtles.* New York: Random House, 1970.

Homer. *The Odyssey.* Trans. Robert Fagles. New York: Viking Penguin, 1996.

Jackson, J. B. *The Necessity of Ruins.* Amherst: University of Massachusetts Press, 1980.

Klemperer, Victor. *I Will Bear Witness: A Diary of the Nazi Years 1942–1945.* Trans. Martin Chalmers. New York: Random House, 1999.

Lee, Laurie. *I Can't Stay Long.* London: Penguin Books, 1977.

Li Po. *The Selected Poems of Li Po.* Trans. David Hinton. New York: New Directions, 1996.

McAlexander, Hubert H. *Peter Taylor: A Writer's Life.* Baton Rouge: Louisiana State University Press, 2001.

McMurtry, Larry. *Paradise.* New York: Simon & Schuster, 2001.

McMurtry, Larry. *Duane's Depressed.* New York: Simon & Schuster, 1999.

Metzker, Ray K. *Ray K. Metzker: Landscapes.* Essay "Voyage of Discovery" by Evan H. Turner. New York: Aperture, 2000.

Mitchell, Stephen, ed. and trans. *The Selected Poetry of Rainer Maria Rilke.* New York: Random House, 1982.

Modiano, Patrick. *Dora Bruder.* Trans. Joanne Kilmartin. Berkeley: University of California Press, 1999.

Naipaul, V. S. *The Enigma of Arrival.* New York: Alfred A. Knopf, 1987.

Naipaul, V. S. *Half a Life.* New York: Alfred A. Knopf, 2001.

Noyes, Russell, ed. *English Romantic Poetry and Prose.* New York: Oxford University Press, 1956.

Olds, Bruce. *Bucking the Tiger.* New York: Farrar, Straus and Giroux, 2001.

Phra Prayudh Payatto. *Buddhadhamma: Natural Laws and Values for Life.* Trans. Grant A. Olson. Albany: State University of New York Press, 1995.

Quinney, Laura. *The Poetics of Disappointment: Wordsworth to Ashbery.* Charlottesville: University Press of Virginia, 1999.

Quinney, Richard. *Borderland: A Midwest Journal.* Madison: University of Wisconsin Press, 2001.

Quinney, Richard. *For the Time Being: Ethnography of Everyday Life.* Albany: State University Press of New York, 1998.

Quinney, Richard. *Journey to a Far Place: Autobiographical Reflections.* Philadelphia: Temple University Press, 1991.

Rorem, Ned. *Lies: A Diary, 1986 – 1999.* Washington, D.C.: Counterpoint, 2000.

Seung Sahn. *Only Don't Know.* Boston: Shambhala, 1999 (1982).

Shunryu Suzuki. *Zen Mind, Beginner's Mind.* New York: Weatherhill, 1970.

Taylor, Peter. *Summons to Memphis.* New York: Alfred A. Knopf, 1986.

Teale, Edwin Way. *A Walk Through the Year.* New York: Dodd, Mead, 1978.

Travis, David. *Edward Weston: The Last Years in Carmel.* Chicago: Art Institute of Chicago, 2001.

Vendler, Helen. *The Art of Shakespeare's Sonnets.* Cambridge: Harvard University Press, 1997.

Watts, Isaac. *The Psalms and Hymns of Isaac Watts.* Morgan, PA: Soli Deo Gloria, 1997 (1719).

Wenders, Wim. *Once: Pictures and Stories.* New York: Distributed Art Publishers, 2001.

Wescott, Glenway. *Good-Bye Wisconsin.* New York: Harper, 1928.

Wright, Charles. *The World of Ten Thousand Things, Poems 1980 – 1990.* New York: Farrar, Straus and Giroux, 1990.

Zimmer, Paul. *Crossing to the Sunlight: Selected Poems.* Athens: University of Georgia Press, 1996.

Acknowledgments

AS ON A WINE-DARK SEA, our crew sailed through the year of 2001. It was an odyssey that could not have been completed without the steady guidance and support of my fellow travelers. Comfort was given to me during the year of struggle with leukemia by my friends and colleagues Mickey Braswell, Bud Brown, Paul and Mari Jo Buhle, Marshall Clinard, David Friedrichs, Sue Guarino-Ghezzi, Clinton Jesser, Rick Jones, David Kobrin, George Kourvetaris, Dragan Milovanovic, Don Noel and Sally O'Connor, Heinz Osterle, Hal Pepinsky, Derek Phillips, Jack Rhoads, Randy Shelden, Dennis Sullivan, Chuck Terry, Jim Thomas, Larry Tifft, Javier Trevino, Gordon Tuffli, Estelle Von Zellen, and John Wozniak. My neighbors Al and Cele Meyer and my friends Norm Engstrom and Kevin Anderson kept a close and much appreciated watch. I was in the thoughts and prayers of my cousins — Joyce Dougherty, Gail and Dale Folkers, and Dean and Shirley Taylor. For the love and attention known in families, I give thanks to my daughters Laura and Anne, my son-in law Billy, my grandsons Daniel and Julian, my stepchildren — Bob, Alene, Karen, Billy, Krissy, and their families—and my brother Ralph and sister-in-law Lois and their family. Solveig my wife cared for me daily and with love brought me safely through the year. Together we traveled night and day the odyssey 2001. I know the blessing of my good fortune.

For comments and advice in the writing of this book, I thank Jerry Apps, Ron Berger, Steve Delchamps, Norman Denzin, and Mark Vinz. I thank Paul Clark for printing my photographs and Ken Crocker for designing the book. And I am grateful for the continuing care provided by my doctor, hematologist Eliot Williams.

My story extends far beyond the individual life. I hope my writing will be of help to others. Dawn with her rose-red fingers comes again for another day.

About the Author

Richard Quinney is the author of several books that combine autobiographical writing and photography, including *Journey to a Far Place, For the Time Being, Borderland,* and *Once Again the Wonder.* His other books are in the academic field of sociology. He and his wife live in Madison, Wisconsin and on the family farm in Walworth County.

This book is set in Adobe Garamond, a digital interpretation by Robert Slimbach of the sixteenth-cen-
tury roman types of Claude Garamond and the italic
types of Robert Granjon. It was designed by Ken
Crocker and printed and bound at The Stinehour
Press. The paper is Cougar Vellum.